STUFF MOM NEVER TOLD YOU

THE FEMINIST PAST, PRESENT, AND FUTURE

ANNEY REESE & SAMANTHA McVEY

STUFF
YOU
SHOULD
READ

'An
iHeart
Book

FLATIRON
BOOKS
NEW YORK

www.flatironbooks.com

The Library of Congress Cataloging-in-Publication Data is available upon request.

ISBN 978-1-250-26860-0 (paper over board)
ISBN 978-1-250-26861-7 (ebook)

Our books may be purchased in bulk for promotional, educational, or business
use. Please contact your local bookseller or the Macmillan Corporate and
Premium Sales Department at 1-800-221-7945, extension 5442, or by email at
MacmillanSpecialMarkets@macmillan.com.

First Edition: 2023

10 9 8 7 6 5 4 3 2 1

STUFF MOM NEVER TOLD YOU

SAMANTHA

ANNEY

TO ALL THE FRIENDS AND FAMILY
WHO SUPPORTED US AND ALL
THE INTERSECTIONAL FEMINISTS
WHO MADE THIS POSSIBLE.

CONT

AUTHORS' NOTE

WRITING A BOOK about feminism is daunting. Writing a disclaimer about writing a book about feminism is also daunting.

Sitting down to write this book is far more daunting than the five podcasts we create every week. When the podcast *Stuff Mom Never Told You* launched over ten years ago with the goal of examining everything and anything through a feminist lens, the social landscape was very different. Since then, the show has evolved just as our conversations have. The voices have changed (literally—we took over the podcast from the wonderful former hosts midstride and had to figure out how to fill some very large shoes!), and over time, we've become more confident in ourselves and more willing to take risks and to highlight issues—and celebrate amazing women—we find particularly important. It's been an awe-inspiring process.

A continual audio format gives us space to grow each and every week, to tailor our topics to the issues of the day, to take listener feedback, and to adapt and address those questions and concerns. A book, by contrast, feels much more final. We know we won't have a chance for a redo if we get anything wrong.

In writing this book, we had a lot of decisions to make, and let me tell you, they weren't easy. It required choosing moments and people and organizations, when there is *so much* to choose from, and then fretting over what those choices communicated. We hoped to present something new, highlighting things and people you may never have heard of. Or perhaps you have, but not necessarily in this context. In doing so, we did our best to offer some perspective as to why we made these choices, and why they are, just like everything, problematic.

We wanted to do our best to encompass many stories of intersectional feminism, but no community is a monolith. Every event we've picked out has a conversation around it, of pros and cons, of what it truly represented and who it helped, especially in terms of a patriarchal, white supremacist, cis-heteronormative system. We included these conversations in here to the best of our ability, in this format, with our own experiences in mind. But of course, there are experts out there—real experts, not podcasters!—and folks with lived experiences different from ours. And they are well worth seeking out, in order to continue expanding your feminist understanding.

In choosing these moments, we want to emphasize we are not claiming these specific ones to be the most important ones, or the only piece of any one story. They are pieces of a larger puzzle, sometimes confounding pieces, and no one agrees where they should go. We found ourselves asking, Geez, why did we choose so many things from the '70s??? Or the '90s??? Well, most likely they coincide with different waves of feminism, and the ideas and subjects we grew up learning about, probably.

Another thing to note: we did primarily focus on Western feminism, mostly because we are aware that we are not the best ones to discuss feminism in contexts we did not grow up with. We have not studied these topics widely outside our own country, though we would love to read as many of those books as we can one day, about how feminism has evolved in other countries and cultures, so we can learn and grow and expand our own perspectives.

We also want to acknowledge that, as a part of these conversations, there are ongoing discussions about terminology and evolving understandings of all these issues. That's a bit frightening in terms of writing a book as well, but it's healthy and necessary. In a month, in a year, in five years, much in this book is likely going to feel dated—possibly even offensive or ignorant. We shudder to think so, but it's true. We believe that we are up to the task of evolving our own thinking, constantly and forever, and hopefully revising this book someday to reflect that.

We acknowledge, too, that not everything in the pages that follow is easy. So much of it isn't. So much of it is brutal to revisit, in truth. In light of that, we have a rating system for each chapter, in terms of how difficult you might find the topics tackled within. The ratings are subjective, but we've done our best to give you the tools to take care of yourself.

As daunting as all these disclaimers add up to be, we do find something telling and almost comforting in their makeup. No one person or event accounts for all of intersectional feminism. It has taken and continues to take so many people of all backgrounds fighting often thankless fights, building off each other and supporting each other.

We (as in the royal *we*) don't always succeed, and the work is rarely easy. We acknowledge that there has long been an issue, historically but also recently, of white feminism tending to exclude others. There are also far too many instances to count of women of color, and particularly Black women of color, not getting credit for their work and their ideas. These are things we cannot and should not ignore. These are things that, if not addressed, will harm us all.

But all these complications might help you understand why the decisions of whom and what to highlight in these pages were so difficult to make. All we hope is that in the book that follows, we're putting together a beautiful puzzle, one that remains incomplete. Or perhaps we're helping weave a strong and durable tapestry across time, with so many hands helping, and so much more work to do.

INTRODUCTION

 T TOOK ME A LONG TIME to claim the label *feminist*. I grew up in a small, conservative town. As someone who identified as female, I wasn't allowed to take auto shop in school like I wanted— I had to take home economics. In middle school, a teacher told me privately that I should not continue excelling at math if I ever wanted to get a boyfriend. In high school, I had a teacher who had a policy that the boys had to get the class textbooks for the girls, a policy that infuriated me to no end. I saw it as a waste of time, and the implications annoyed me. One day I'd had enough and grabbed a book off the shelf myself, mostly out of annoyance rather than any need to make a big statement. The boy getting books from the shelf sneered, "Anney, are you a feminist?"

The whole class went absolutely silent, waiting for my answer. And me? I froze, absolutely panicked. In my high school mind, I knew claiming such a label would be a social death sentence. Eventually I mustered something up about how it was such a waste of time, but my classmates didn't let up, asking me if I shaved my legs, if I wore makeup, if I wore a bra, if I in fact hated men, and if that is why I didn't have a boyfriend. You know. That tired old feminist caricature that has been weaponized for so long.

My answers to questions like these were enough to dismiss myself as a bad feminist, someone who had no right to the label at all. I did and do shave, wear makeup, and wear a bra (though less so to all those things during the pandemic). The implication (and my extremely flawed understanding of) the "good feminist" answer to those questions kept me quiet.

Later, when I entered the professional world and started seeing articles advising women on how to be taken more seriously at work, I shrank even further. *Don't use exclamation marks in emails*—I do!!! *Don't say sorry*—I do! ☹ *Oh, don't use emojis.* ☹☹ *Don't ever bring baked goods*—but I like cooking for people! This embarrassed me, as if by doing all these things, I was sending the message loud and clear that I was not, nor could I ever be, a feminist.

There is so much problematic, toxic stuff to untangle when it comes to why I felt that way, and a lot of it is more nuanced than I have time to go into here. But essentially, it boils down to me feeling ashamed of things that are more associated with being feminine and that participating in those things disqualified me from feminism. That unless I was *a perfect feminist*, I would be seen as a phony and dismissed.

But wait. *There is no such thing as a perfect feminist.* That is not an excuse to not recognize where we fall short, and learn and grow from those experiences, and always try to be better.

And all those behaviors I mentioned? They are far more complicated than *you should do this* or *you shouldn't do that*. They all have histories, many of which are rooted in capitalist ad campaigns to make women feel inadequate in their bodies so they'll buy a product. Or they are rooted in our long history of limiting women to unpaid or underpaid and disrespected spheres of domesticity. Or of punishing women for taking up space and being ambitious while rewarding men for being aggressive under the same circumstances.

It's hard work to unlearn all the toxic messaging you've been bombarded with growing up. It isn't easy to start sorting out what you do—is it because you want to, or is it because it's what you've been socialized with? The answers so often will be a mix of both.

All this is further complicated by our own experiences and intersections. Feminism doesn't have the best track record of being inclusive, though in recent years, we are seeing a lot of conversations about this issue, and there is some growth as we all push feminism toward a better, more inclusive space. Of course, it heartens me to see this growth, in the movement and in others as well, though I know we still have a lot of work to do.

I REMEMBER HAVING a conversation with a roommate in college about what we wanted in life and the things we were hoping to achieve. And though it sounds like a cliché, I remember her talking about the fact she didn't really care about getting her degree, how she was basically just waiting until she could get married and start her adult life.

And, honestly, that wasn't a big deal to me. I mean our whole adolescence and teen years were filled with the notion that we were looking for the "one" so we could start living the perfect life. Somehow our conversation soon turned to the subject of women and careers. Suddenly, that word *feminism* came out. Her response? She told me she didn't believe in feminism and would never call herself a feminist.

Of course, me being me and truly not understanding why she would say such a thing, I was shocked and asked her why. But she didn't really have an explanation. I let her know that if it hadn't been for feminism, she wouldn't have been able to come to school at all and that she would have been shunned for not having already gotten married in her early twenties. The conversation didn't last much longer.

My old friend has since grown and matured—I mean, haven't we all? But to be honest, my response to her back then, though not entirely incorrect, was nowhere near complete. And the conversation has stayed with me. Why? I think it's because the word *feminism* has, since the beginning, been such a controversial one that I started to wonder if I truly understood it. And, you know what? Turns out, I didn't.

 ONE THING SAMANTHA and I find useful in our podcast is to establish working definitions, so we are on the same page. Perhaps the most important of those is the definition of *intersectional feminism*, which we will cover in more depth later in the book. But for now, you just need to know that lawyer, activist, and intersectional feminist Kimberlé Crenshaw coined the term *intersectionality* in 1989 as, she says, "a prism for seeing the way in which various forms of inequality often operate together and exacerbate each other . . . All inequality is not created equal."

According to Crenshaw:

An intersectional approach shows the way that people's social identities can overlap, creating compounding experiences of discrimination. We tend to talk about race inequality as separate from inequality based on gender, class, sexuality, or immigrant status. What's often missing is how some people are subject to all of these, and the experience is not just the sum of its parts.

At its core, the concept of intersectionality is an intentional, cognizant mindset that acknowledges that our identities—of race, of gender, of disability, of sexual orientation, and so on—cannot be separated out. They are all important in terms of equality, which is what feminism ultimately is about. The feminist movement has often been fragmented and exclusionary, but intersectionality is starting to address that, with the understanding that exclusionary feminism isn't truly feminism and that we are stronger when we stand together.

MY PREVIOUS CAREER, before starting to work on this podcast, was in child services and juvenile justice. That work opened my eyes to the depth and darkness of the patriarchy, but I didn't know what that term referred to yet either. And I hadn't even started to recognize the deeply ingrained misogyny that I had been carrying around myself. But the biases I didn't think I had became more and more apparent as I grew in my journey.

Working in a field that seeks to improve the lives of others and to advocate for them was important for me. But to my surprise, it was through my new life working on this podcast that I have been able to see and discover so much more. Sometimes it feels overwhelming because every day I realize that I have so much more to learn. But I also know how important it is to keep going. The last few years have highlighted how little progress we've made, or maybe, more accurately, how much progress we've made but just how precarious it all is. And I guess progress comes in cycles—we step forward, we are pulled back, and we link arms to push forward once more.

Looking around right now, the policies and policymakers that threaten our autonomy—as people with uteruses, as marginalized communities—feel as much of a threat as they have ever been. Honestly? It's exhausting.

WHEN I STARTED working as a producer on *Stuff Mom Never Told You* just out of college, it was eye-opening to me. It put into words things I had felt but never truly acknowledged or knew how to describe, that I'd never heard discussed in my small hometown. It gave me history and context and the tools to understand the things I felt as a woman every day. It made me ask more questions; it forced me to learn more about myself and those around me.

It's still an eye-opening experience. There is so much yet to learn and so many ways to do better. And that's one of the reasons we wrote this book—to continue our own education and perhaps to expand yours as well.

With this book, we hope to bring to light lesser-known stories of the people who have done the work, people who should have been getting the accolades and attention but didn't. We wanted to embark on an educational thought experiment—if this intersectional event hadn't happened, then what? Through that, we wanted to educate ourselves and others on the importance and impact of these events, while honoring those who have paved the way for us. We also hope to underline how much work is left to be done.

We really wanted to make the book an immersive and engaging experience, and we were fortunate enough to convince a super-talented local Atlanta artist, Helen Choi, to work with us. And she made our wildest dreams come true—creating beautiful illustrations for the text to help us tell these stories. Some chapters are more straightforward history lessons; others are a bit of fiction mixed with nonfiction to help us understand the impact of some of the biggest moments in the feminist movement and what our world might be like if they had never happened. Throughout, there are games and challenges and lots of did-you-knows. And obviously, anyone who knows me knows I couldn't help but talk about Princess Leia and other fictional women, so buckle up for that as well!

TO BE HONEST, the work that Anney and I do every day makes me anxious. It causes me to doubt myself, not only as a podcaster but as a feminist. There's an implication that what we talk about or what we think is important is us just playing at being social justice warriors, that we're spouting off without really doing the work. Is it all just performative?

Truthfully, I sometimes question if that is what we are doing. Are we making it worse? Are we bad examples? Are we making the ones who have paved this path for us proud? What will be our legacy? This line of questioning can bring out so much negativity in myself—I mean, am I even worthy to help write this book? Who am I to tell the story of these historic events or highlight these amazing folks?

Then I think about all the feminists who have held back because they were afraid of not being perfect, who shunned the label because they felt they were not worthy of it. Of all the progress and sisterhood lost because of these very doubts. Fear of failure, of not being enough, kept me from contributing to my full potential for a long time, and it still haunts me. Now I try to face these doubts head-on, knowing that I will fall down, but I will get back up, dust myself off, and grow. I still have so much left to learn and I'm excited to do so. I am one of many feminists, and all our stories are valuable.

The feminists who came before me have made a difference; in large and small ways, they have left an imprint. Those who will come long after me will do so as well. And that's something that has been a foundation of both our podcast and our goal with this book: to remember that our voices matter, and to remind you that your voice matters, no matter the level of impact.

Fear has kept women silent for a long time. We have been silenced, because those in power worry that if we dare to be visible, we will destroy the system that has been set to keep us down. As a woman of color, I have been taught that my fears should control me, but that isn't true. I refuse to let that be true. Throughout history, we have seen those who stepped out of the shadows, tired of remaining invisible. We have been witness to their refusal to submit to the status quo. These brave women—the revolutionaries—understood what it means to be human, to make mistakes, to learn from them, and to continue to grow.

We know all too well what it feels like to make mistakes. We have made them on the show, no doubt, and we were scared to write a book and risk doing it again. But over time, we have also learned the value of moving forward with purpose—to learn from our mistakes, to acknowledge and correct our wrongs, to take responsibility for the words we speak and the actions we take. I know that those wrongs are how I learn, by asking questions, by fixing mistakes, by learning to listen to others about their own experiences, their own worldview, their own truths.

> Fear has kept women silent for a long time.

We understand we have a huge responsibility as feminists to grow with the movement. We must acknowledge that history tends to repeat itself when there are experiences and voices that were ignored before. These omissions must be corrected. We know that our responsibility is not to know everything but to keep learning, to keep growing.

This book is something that, I hope, expresses our curiosity, our humility, our growth, and above all, our optimism. We hope you will come with us on this journey, so we can learn and grow as feminists, together.

STUFF
MOM
NEVER
TOLD
YOU

THE HERO

NAME: Princess General Leia Organa

BIO: Daughter of Padmé Naberrie Amidala and Jedi Anakin Skywalker/Darth Vader, twin sister to Jedi Luke Skywalker. Senator as a teenager. Leader in the Rebellion against the Empire as a teenager. Faced off against one of the most terrifying villains, Darth Vader (surprise, he's your father!) and held her ground. Lost her planet. Kept the Alliance going when everything was absolutely dire. Rescued her man. Got married, had a kid, helped rebuild a democratic government, kept fighting, kept leading, never gave up hope.

RELEVANT QUOTE: "Aren't you a little short for a stormtrooper?"

FICTIONAL WOMEN PRESENTS

BIGGER PICTURE

STORIES MATTER. What we see and hear as a child influences how we think the world operates and what we think we can become within it. Who can be the hero?

Representation within stories matters. Numerous studies have proven that representation not only impacts the worldviews of children but also influences government policy. If people perceive something to be true, based on the media they consume, then lawmakers (who, yes, are also people) will act on that too.

People have been telling stories since the beginning of humanity. To share wisdom, teach a lesson, form connections, laugh, cry. The act of storytelling is powerful, whether it's through oral tradition, paintings, sculptures, books, comics, television, movies, or video games.

The characters in these stories matter. We connect with them. And when it comes to the hero, we want them to succeed. To see some part of ourselves in them. That can be hard when a traditional "hero" looks one certain way.

Who is writing these stories matters too. Different voices and perspectives are essential to creating a diverse roster of heroes that resonate, that make us all feel like we could put on the cape ourselves and become the hero of our own story.

WHY SHE MATTERS TO ME

Let me tell you about Leia Organa, leader, badass, fashion icon, hero, and one of the loves of my life. She has taken up residence in my heart, sending out such deep roots that I doubt she'll ever be dislodged. Her influence will forever live within me.

I don't remember a time before I saw *Star Wars*. One of my very first memories is of watching *The Empire Strikes Back*. I remember staring up at Leia as she confidently commanded men heads taller than her. It was never a question that, just because she was a woman, she couldn't be in command. She had a small stature, but it never seemed to matter. She had a presence that immediately demanded respect, a voice that was sharp, firm, and sometimes even snarky.

Leia is the only character mentioned in the opening crawl of the first-produced *Star Wars* movie, 1977's *A New Hope*. She has the best introduction of any character of the original series, fight me. When we first meet her, she is *already* a hero. She's a leader of the rebellion, a senator, incredibly capable, even at the young age of *nineteen*. Leia is the one that sets up all the action.

We're meant to believe she is a damsel in distress, waiting for rescue, but she immediately rewrites the story we're expecting. When Luke Skywalker first enters her prison cell disguised

"AND ANOTHER THING!"

 An offshoot of the hero is, of course, the superhero. I grew up reading comics. I would seek out girls and women to read about, but those kinds of stories weren't always easy to find. Many of the standard plotlines involved pregnancy, infertility, and rape; the comics were clearly written more to "other" the women in these stories, to put their bodies at the forefront, and always via the male gaze.

It was always there, an unspoken footnote: "But she's a woman." Often the woman in these comics needed saving; she served as the damsel in distress to further the (more important, of course) male hero's story.

And the outfits. Seriously, go look up some of the early superhero outfits that were designed for fictional women. You can marvel at these costumes and how incredibly sexualized and *nonfunctional* they are. I'm all for dressing sexily

and feeling good about yourself, but this was not that. *This* was reminding people that the intended audience was boys and men, and that the women were objects to be ogled and often mocked. She's so cute, she thinks she can play with the boys in essentially her bra and underwear, willfully ignoring the fact the (mostly male) illustrators and writers designed these outfits.

Because these outfits are objectively nonfunctional when it comes to fighting supervillains, the message is that these female superheroes aren't really there to be superheroes. That perhaps their superpower is seducing men in a patriarchal society, which reduces these characters to pawns in a misogynistic system.

While there has been so much progress, we still have a long way to go. Female-led superhero movies are still news, as are superhero movies featuring nonwhite folks and containing queer storylines—but at least they are entering the mainstream for the first time, slowly but surely.

But let us not detract from the fact there are and have been amazing women creators and characters in the comic book space, and the number is growing. True, they do not get as much attention or backing from big studios, though that, too, is starting to change. Often, I feel like I have to put in far more work to find storylines crafted by women, and when I do discover them, I'm angry that more people don't know about these stunning, heartfelt, and creative stories. Of course, this all comes with the caveat that indie comic books are also lovely, and not everyone wants that big publisher or studio contract, but we can't deny those stories get more eyes and ears. Companies are gradually taking note of this with Black- and female-led films like *Black Panther* and *Captain Marvel*, not to mention an increase in queer characters, like in recent additions to the Thor franchise, but progress is frustratingly halting in many respects. Further, many of these companies do not provide the same support for these properties, especially when it comes to the online abuse heaped on the participants and creators. Even the merchandising options are subpar. Yes, it is changing. But ever so slowly.

I have been literally moved to tears when enjoying stories that depict women in the lead, women working together, women supporting each other, or at diverse storylines told genuinely. That is the power of these stories—the power of representation. Representation isn't everything, but it is a big part of the picture. As we know, children interpret the world and their roles within it based on what they see in front of them—when they see faces and hear stories like their own, a new realm of possibilities opens to them. Studies have found that consuming entertainment where people can see themselves not only impacts what they think *they* can do but also what they believe is possible for others.

as an enemy stormtrooper in hopes of being her hero, she is ready with a witty comment. When Luke's poorly thought out, fantasy-fueled rescue plan falls through, she's the one who takes charge. She's brash and strong and smart and passionate and feminine and funny; she is both a princess and a leader, someone people respect and follow, someone who gets things done. She's both the steadfast organizer and the knight in shining armor Luke mistakenly assumed he'd be for her, only to have the tables turned on him. It's Luke Skywalker and Han Solo who

The world was introduced to Princess Leia during second-wave feminism.

need to figure out what it means to be a hero. Leia's journey is figuring out how to honor her own personal wants, because she is *already the hero*.

And Leia is the hero who stays. Han leaves. Luke leaves. Leia is the one who stays on to lead the fight against evil

forces and bestow advice on the younger generation.

It's hard to quantify how much of an impact the Princess Leia character had on girls and women around the world, but the word *huge* is a gross understatement. When the great, incomparable Carrie Fisher died, the internet was flooded with posts from people of all backgrounds, passionate about how important this character and Fisher's portrayal of her was to them. At protests all around the world, people brandish signs of her as a symbol of rebellion against misogyny and sexism. Leia went on to inspire so many other fictional female characters we love today, characters that little girls look up to.

Back when these movies came out—and even now, though to a lesser extent—a character like Leia was rare. The world was introduced to Princess Leia during second-wave feminism—when women were fighting for abortion rights, the sexual revolution was in full swing, and women were entering the workplace in force. Here was this fictional woman, the leader of it all and too unyielding to be questioned about it. She's feminine,

a damn fashion icon, someone who has moments of vulnerability but is occupying a masculine space with a sharp, cutting grace that dares you to tell her she shouldn't be there.

And I was a young girl watching this, living in a world that seemed to constantly tell me that *I* shouldn't be there.

For so long, the dichotomy has been hero = man, princess = woman, one who always needs to be rescued by her hero. Princess (and later General) Leia challenged that. I feel so lucky now, having her growing up. There's no part of these movies that questions she's a badass, a force to be reckoned with. She just *is*. Immediately and always.

Yes, yes, I can hear your questions now. But what about her relationship with Han Solo? But what about some of the stuff that went on during filming? What about the gold bikini, Anney? WHAT ABOUT THE GOLD BIKINI???

[Oh, I have thoughts. So many thoughts. Who killed Jabba? Leia, with the chains of her oppression!!! But this is not that book, though if you'd like to learn more, I have talked about it at length on the podcast . . .]

People are hungrier for stories than ever, and if the popularity of franchises like *Star Wars* and the Marvel Cinematic Universe are any indicator, our love of the hero's journey is not going away anytime soon. But we're also hungry for stories that are more representative and diverse, more like *us*.

Characters like Leia's paved the way for more characters like her to be written, to be celebrated, to even exist. But this shift has not been without significant and disheartening backlash. Actors portraying women and people of color in popular movie franchises are getting death threats, and their movies are being review-bombed. More often than not, heroic characters—especially the ones who are accepted, who are revered—are white and cis-hetero. These spaces in particular—science fantasy, science fiction, and comics—have traditionally been viewed as male spaces and thus, they are gatekept, even though women have been at the forefront of these worlds since the beginning.

I would argue that this male-first mindset—especially coupled with the hardcore gendering of

merchandise that was going on in the 1980s when *Return of the Jedi* came out—in part explains why Princess Leia even wore that damn gold bikini: *She can be in our male space, but only under our rules and for our pleasure.*

It's interesting that although what's happening in that scene is supposed to be horrendous, that Jabba is a gross, monstrous villain and Leia is openly contemptuous of him—and that both this outfit and this scene received a mere two minutes of screen time—audiences at large still labeled the moment as "sexy." (And yes, according to Carrie Fisher, the filming conditions allowed no room for dignity.)

We see this narrative play out over and over again in fan culture, whether in video games or comic books or movies like *Star Wars*. More space is made for marginalized folks, then comes the backlash. The gatekeeping. The determination of entitled fans, often white men, to signal that, in their minds, they own this space, and you will play by their rules—*put on that damn gold bikini and like it*—or get out. Two steps forward, one step back. We're seeing a growth in more diverse storylines in recent

years, and the sadly predictable and horrendous backlash that follows, telling marginalized folks, *You don't belong here. You're not welcome.* Big companies and social media platforms have been slow to crack down on this, and we should push them to do better. But marginalized folks have always been here and we're not going away. And now, we are no longer willing to be here under misogynistic, racist, homophobic, and ableist rules.

You wouldn't believe how often I've been aggressively quizzed at comic conventions by men as if I'm not a "real" fan, accused of pretending, merely so I can get a boyfriend or get hit on. If I pass their tests, then they tell me I'm not like other girls. But guess what? I am! Girls and women *do* like comics and science fiction and science fantasy and all kinds of things really. This toxic behavior, and the fact that historically, women *have* been the sexualized damsel in distress—a tool to further the male hero's storyline (and often killed off for their trouble)—has understandably turned women and marginalized folks away or encouraged them to keep their interests to themselves. This

"AND ANOTHER THING!"

 Let's talk briefly about the feminism of the male character Luke Skywalker, another love of my life. For our purposes we are sticking to the original trilogy here because otherwise I'm going to give everyone, myself included, a headache. Leia is pretty masculine-coded for a female character, especially given her bluntness and commitment issues. At the same time, Luke, a male hero in a science fantasy series, is quite a bit more balanced when it comes to traditionally feminine and masculine traits, with some even arguing that he is essentially a *feminine-coded* character, or at least in the stereotypical sense. (Did you know that Luke, or the very early version of his character, was originally written as female?)

While Luke Skywalker has plenty of traditionally masculine-coded traits—hot-headedness, recklessness, that whole I-have-to-be-the-hero vibe— he's balanced out with quite a few feminine-coded traits, including empathy, compassion, loyalty, and kindness. He's also relatively small in stature, far from your typical buff male superhero.

You can take this line of thinking even further when you notice how Luke in particular interacts with the Force. You've got Obi-Wan and Yoda telling him he has to confront his father, Darth Vader, to become a Jedi, like his father once was. You've got Luke saying he can't do it, because he so strongly believes—he can *feel* it—that there is still good in Darth Vader (Luke's mother's dying words echoed this sentiment). He's being emotional here, isn't he? This is a critique most often lobbed at women.

Then, after Luke turns himself over to Vader, banking on his feelings and hope, Vader turns him over to the Emperor. The Emperor urges him to embrace his destructive anger, give into his aggression, and kill his father. Violence and anger—these are stereotypically masculine traits. When Luke does finally give in, he almost loses himself to the dark side and continues the cycle of violence when he cuts off his father's hand.

But this, in opposition to many more typical hero storylines in our media, is framed as a failure, a weakness on Luke's part. His act of heroism is throwing away his (very phallic) weapon and refusing to fight, not allowing violence and anger to control him. Once again, he is embracing more feminine-coded traits and standing up to the toxic masculinity that demands his aggression, his fury. This act brings out the empathy and love in Darth Vader and finally breaks the cycle.

Luke also rejects the old Jedi order as well as the Empire—in my mind, this is a perfect metaphor for how feminism demands systemic change. The importance of Luke's character can't be understated when it comes to how we understand heroism. Here it is portrayed not as an aggressive display of strength, which is typically coded as masculine, but as an empathetic display of compassion and kindness, which of course is typically coded as feminine. And this is an act of strength in itself. Luke Skywalker = Feminist Hero.

C'mon @ me, Mark Hamill! What's a girl gotta do? Write a book??

phenomenon, and numerous other obstacles, influences what gets made and who tells these stories.

When I was eight years old, with the help of a family friend, I made a Jedi outfit for Halloween for a character I created, inspired by Princess Leia, named Terra Polaris. She was not to be trifled with, and everyone who guessed I was Obi-Wan Kenobi received a proud and excited spiel about the young girl who became a Jedi and all her heroic adventures. It may sound silly, but without characters like Leia, I'm not sure whether my imagination would have placed me in the role of the hero. It makes my heart soar when I see young girls dressed as Leia, or Rey, the female protagonist from the new *Star Wars* trilogy.

That's the power of these stories, the ones we tell and share and pass on. That's why it's important to tell, and support, stories that represent all of us— stories that tell little girls that they can indeed be the hero—or that maybe, just maybe, that they already are one.

CHAPTER 1

BATTLE OF THE SEXES

SMNTY WARNING

I thought it would set us back 50 years if I didn't win that match. It would ruin the women's tour and affect all women's self-esteem.

—BILLIE JEAN KING

- This chapter is rated "I" for "infuriating." But also for "inspiring."

- Brief discussion of sexual assault.

IT WAS A WARM NIGHT AT THE ASTRODOME IN HOUSTON, TEXAS. PEOPLE AROUND THE WORLD TUNED INTO THE MUCH HYPED "BATTLE OF THE SEXES" TENNIS MATCH BETWEEN BOBBY RIGGS AND BILLIE JEAN KING.

IT'S STARTING!!! BILLIE JEAN IS GOING TO WHOOP BOBBY RIGGS!

CLOSE SCORE, BUT THE FIRST SET GOES TO RIGGS.

OH NO!

HONEY, IT'S JUST AN EXHIBITION MATCH...

MOM, SHE'S WON THE FRENCH OPEN AND THE US OPEN! SHE'S GOING TO WIN THIS!

THE SECOND SET GOES TO KING!

SHE'S GOING TO BE THE CHAMPION!

A CHAMPION.

The girl felt like she'd lost the match alongside Billie Jean King. She felt like the male announcers, like Bobby Riggs, were settling back, smiling and happy, proven right in their minds. Just like the boys she played against. They all believed, truly believed, that girls and women win only when boys and men let them. Those boys didn't have that feeling, that unnamed feeling telling them, *No, no, no. This is not for you.*

The girl couldn't name that feeling, but she knew it too well; she'd known it for what felt like forever, and she hated it. It made her want to make herself small, to be quiet, to hide herself away. She hated how it was always there, even though she didn't want it to be, just waiting to get loud in her mind.

When the boys from the local public courts stopped by to ask her to play again, she refused. They taunted her gently about King's loss, pretending they were kidding but knowing it hurt. The girl acted like it didn't bother her, even made herself believe that tennis was just a passing hobby, like an embarrassing habit that maybe she would grow out of. She scoffed when her mother tried to get her back onto those courts.

King continued to play, even continued to win. But the girl sensed that when people talked about King, they did so dismissively. As if she had already proven herself to be not as good as, no matter what she accomplished from here.

The girl gave up tennis. Her mother gave her tennis clothes away and donated her racket to her old club. She took down the framed copy of King's picture on the cover of the December 25, 1972 issue of *Sports Illustrated*—the first time a woman had even been chosen as Sportsperson of the Year—from her wall.

Occasionally the girl found herself thinking about these items, things that had once been so precious to her, wondering, hoping that another girl had picked them up and, along with them, her dream as well. Perhaps that girl would go on to be an inspiration to others as Billie Jean King had been to her, that this younger, brighter girl would be filled with so much hope and determination, that her kinetic energy wouldn't go unspent. That this imaginary girl might take on the next Bobby Riggs of the world and defeat him.

Sometimes the girl regretted quitting tennis, but as time passed, the loss hurt less. She understood her feelings around it more as she grew older. But she could see that the national discourse had shifted since that match, very much in the way she had feared it would when she was a child, even if she hadn't had the words or tools to articulate it.

She could sense, in the air, that it was easier for the sports world to sit back, comfortable in their self-assured smugness that this was, in fact, the nature of things. That women belonged in the bedroom or the kitchen, not competing at the highest levels of sports. That women can and should be allowed to compete only by the grace of men. *Look at the little lady trying to compete. So sweet she thinks she can win.*

The changes were subtle at first, but hard to miss. It was impossible to find a women's game or match on television, in any sport. Female athletes did not make nearly as much as male athletes did. They were not as respected, not taken seriously. The attitude permeated all sports.

Still, there were women out there who weren't deterred. Who persevered. Who caught national attention, even international attention. But they were rarities.

The girl, now a woman, mourned the girl she had once been, avidly watching the Battle of the Sexes, so full of hope, until Billie Jean King lost and people cheered at her failure. Another woman put in her place; an entire generation assured of the natural order of things.

That women weren't real athletes, and that they couldn't be champions.

BUT THAT'S NOT WHAT HAPPENED

Billie Jean King *didn't* lose the highly anticipated Battle of the Sexes that day in 1973. She won. Definitively and decisively. Some might even say it was a real thrashing. Ninety million people around the globe tuned in to see her win three straight sets (6–4, 6–3, 6–3) against a visibly winded and out-of-shape opponent. Bobby Riggs, who suffered the resounding defeat while wearing his "Sugar Daddy" jacket, was a proud, self-proclaimed chauvinist who once said he believed women belonged in the bed and the kitchen. This one certainly didn't: Billie Jean King was the number one female player in the world both before and after that match—from 1966 through 1968, again from 1971 to 1972, and once more in 1974. Over the course of her career, she earned thirty-nine Grand Slam titles, including twelve singles titles, which puts her seventh on the list of all-time women's singles players.

> I wanted to use sports for social change.
> —BILLIE JEAN KING

The infamous Battle of the Sexes match was hardly the most important match she played—it had no bearing on rankings, after all—yet perhaps it might have been the most historic. It remains the most-watched tennis match in history and one of the most-viewed sporting events of all time.

That day, Billie Jean King took home $100,000 in prize money, while inspiring millions and helping to normalize and encourage sports participation for girls and women for decades to come. After the match, King went on to earn the well-deserved moniker the Mother of Modern Sports.

When presenting Billie Jean King with the Presidential Medal of Freedom in 2012, President Barack Obama said, "You don't realize it, but I saw that match at twelve. And now I have two daughters, and it has made a difference in how I raise them." Parents all over the country would likely echo his sentiment. Data from the 2016 World Economic Forum indicates there has been an almost 1,000 percent increase of women playing high school sports since 1972.

The 1970s was a tumultuous time for social change. Women's liberation was in full swing. *Roe v. Wade* legalized abortion in all fifty states. The Equal Rights Amendment (ERA), ensuring the "equality of rights under the law shall not be denied or abridged by the United States or by any State on account of sex," passed both houses of Congress, was signed by President Richard Nixon, and was sent to the states to ratify. With the help of testimony from Billie Jean King herself, Title IX passed, which prohibited sex discrimination in any educational program that received assistance on the federal level, opening new doors for girls and women in the world of athletics and sports.

After the infamous match, King continued to win, even dominate, and she never stopped fighting for equality and visibility for women in sports. When King received $15,000 less than a man would have for winning the 1972 US Open, she issued an ultimatum to the organizers, saying that unless the winnings were equal by the next year, she and other women were going to stop playing. Believe it or not, the ultimatum worked. The US Open became the first major tournament to offer equal prize money. The next year, in 1973, Billie Jean King founded what was then the only professional coed sports league, World TeamTennis (WTT).

> Althea Gibson was the first woman of color to ever win a major.

That league would have an impact even King might not have been able to imagine. Two children who played matches in the WTT were Serena and Venus Williams. At age ten, Venus was asked to play WTT pro. She later credited King for the opportunity and said, "I intend to keep doing everything I can until Billie Jean's original dream of equality is made real." On top of fighting for equal pay at Wimbledon, Venus also has done grassroots-level work to ensure Black youth have the same opportunities she had.

Venus isn't the only professional tennis player who has spoken out about the influence the King-Riggs match had on their career. Naomi Osaka, Elise Mertens, Martina Navratilova, and Serena Williams have spoken out about it, too, and how it—as well as King's work in general—inspired them to continue pushing for equality in sports.

BREAKING BOUNDARIES

 I can't lie: sports are not one of my strengths. But something I do love is celebrating women who break boundaries, who take hold of something they love and push forward to show other girls that they can step up to break records themselves. So I couldn't resist popping up here to talk about a few women pushing boundaries to become champions in their own right.

OLYMPIC CHAMPION BOXER CLARESSA SHIELDS

Shields is a badass who has won not one but *two* Olympic gold medals, which makes her the only American boxer to win consecutive medals (as of 2021).

Another jaw-dropping accomplishment: Shields is the only boxer—male or female—in history to have claimed all four major world titles in boxing at the same time, in two different weight classes!

Shields also doesn't hold back in calling out the sexism that happens within the sport, nor has she shied away from calling out companies and sponsors in their unwillingness to pay women the same salaries or fees as men. We love a woman who knows her worth!

OLYMPIC SWIMMER KATIE LEDECKY

The 2020 Olympics (or 2021, however you want to look at the weird Covid-delayed Olympics) were a whirlwind for Ledecky. She had us all cheering as she broke records left and right. Having competed since she was fifteen, Ledecky holds three different world records, holds the female record for most gold medals from the Olympics and the World Championships, and has no plans to slow down. She is focused and continues to push as she trains for her next competitions.

TRACK-AND-FIELD STAR WILMA RUDOLPH

As if Rudolph's three Olympic gold medals aren't amazing enough, in 1960 Rudolph was the first American woman to win three gold medals in a *single* Olympic Games. While she was constantly breaking records during her time competing, she was also fighting for her community. Upon returning home from the games, she refused to attend the Olympic parade unless it was integrated.

Rudolph was awarded the Associated Press Female Athlete of the Year award in 1961. Later, she was inducted into the US Olympic Hall of Fame, and in 1990, Rudolph became the first woman to receive the National Collegiate Athletic Association's Silver Anniversary Award.

Rudolph left a legacy for so many young athletes, and not just with her skills. After she stopped competing, she continued to pursue her career in education, teaching athletics to youths in her community after she retired.

King herself was inspired to play by tennis player Althea Gibson: "Althea Gibson was the first woman of color to ever win a major. In '56, she won the French, '57 and '58, she won Wimbledon. I got to see her as a 13-year-old, and she changed my world because I knew what it looked like to be No. 1. She inspired me more than ever."

● ● ● ● ●

King's willingness to fight extended well beyond the world of sports. In 1981, she went public with the fact that she was homosexual, and she became increasingly vocal in the fight for LGBTQ+ rights, even though it reportedly cost her millions in endorsements. King retired from professional tennis in 1984, but she did not stop being a voice and advocate for women athletes.

Some might argue that sports seems like a frivolous thing to talk about when it comes to women's rights and feminism. But a little digging into the history shows otherwise. Sports have always existed at the intersection of sexism, racism, ableism, homophobia, and class prejudice. For millennia, women have fought for parity in sports competition, and even for the right just to play at all. Billie Jean King and Bobby Riggs may have played in the most well-known battle of the sexes, but this was far from the only one.

At the time, King said publicly that she felt an enormous pressure to win the Battle of the Sexes. That she believed if she hadn't won, it would have set women back fifty years. This match was incredibly hyped—it went viral well before the internet existed. It was one match, but to the millions of people watching, it represented so much more. Perhaps this was due in part to increasing social anxiety around all the changes taking place at a time when it came to gender normative scripts, to what women *could* do and what they *should* do.

But this fight isn't a new one, not at all. In fact, women have been fighting to be included in the world of sports for more than a century. Going all the way back to the early days of the modern Olympics, women weren't allowed to compete, although they did have their own separate athletic events. In the 1880s, when the modern iteration of the Olympics and the International Olympic

Committee, or the IOC, was formed by a Frenchman named Baron Pierre de Coubertin, it was a similar time of social shift. It was around that time the term *feminism* itself was coined by French activist Hubertine Auclert.

As you might imagine, the very idea of feminism, especially in the world of sports, met strident opposition. Baron de Coubertin, just like Riggs, resisted women's progress vocally and brashly. He is quoted as saying that the Olympics were created for "the solemn and periodic exaltation of male athleticism" with "female applause as reward." He also lamented that it would be "indecent that spectators should be exposed to the risk of seeing the body of a woman being smashed before their eyes. Besides, no matter how toughened a sportswoman may be, her organism is not cut out to sustain certain shocks. Her nerves rule her muscles, nature wanted it that way." Ugh.

It is no surprise, then, that Coubertin vociferously opposed women competing in the Olympics, claiming, disingenuously, that since no women competed in the ancient Olympics, they should not compete in the modern Olympics either. Despite his and others' protestations, women did compete, albeit unofficially, in the 1900 Olympics, making up 22 of the 997 competitors. They competed in golf, tennis, equestrian events, sailing, and croquet, though only golf and tennis had all-women's events. That year, when Margaret Abbott medaled in golf, she became the first American woman to win an Olympic event.

> Exercising for women was believed to mess with their reproductive organs.

But, the argument went, women didn't belong in the sporting sphere. According to Coubertin, the Victorian woman was not supposed to sweat. She was not supposed to be muscular. Exercising for women was believed to mess with their reproductive organs, something particularly amplified during menstruation or pregnancy. It was deemed unsafe and unladylike for women to participate in sports, at a time when gender norms were never to be broken. Sports that were more acceptable for women to play involved less running around, and the uniforms were very feminine in nature.

But if Coubertin was an 1800s version of Bobby Riggs, there was an 1800s version of Billie Jean King to meet him. This person was French activist and feminist Alice Milliat. During her era, first-wave feminism, and the backlash to it, was in full swing. The Nineteenth Amendment, which granted women the right to vote in the US, passed in 1919. In 1921, Milliat submitted an official request to the IOC to allow women to compete in track-and-field events and decided to host her own Olympics. In 1922, Milliat helped put on the Women's Olympic Games in Paris, with the intent of modeling her event after the four-year schedule of the Olympics. Five countries competed, and the event drew twenty-thousand spectators, as well as the ire of the IOC and Coubertin. They decreed that only the IOC could govern track-and-field events; they went on to prohibit women from competing in these events in the 1924 Olympics.

The show went on. Milliat compromised, striking the word *Olympics* from the name of their event, renaming it the Women's World Games for their competition in 1926, which took place in Gothenburg, Sweden. Once again, these games were a success, drawing large crowds and competitors from nine countries. Finally, the IOC budged, just a bit, allowing women to compete in five track-and-field events in the 1928 Olympic Games. This was, of course, no match for the twenty-two events the men could compete in.

Yet even the fact that women could compete at all in these events led to a caustic reaction among the press. Stories eviscerated these women, pointing to them as proof that women weren't meant to compete. Here's a quote from a story that ran in the *New York Times* about the 1928 games:

> The final of the women's 800-meter run, in which Frau Lina Radke of Germany set a world's record, plainly demonstrated that even this distance makes too great a call on feminine strength. At the finish, six out of the nine runners were completely exhausted and fell headlong on the ground. Several had to be carried off the track. The little American girl, Miss Florence MacDonald, who made a gallant try but was outclassed, was in a half faint for several minutes, while even the sturdy Miss Hitomi of Japan, who finished second, needed attention before she was able to leave the field.

The *New-York Evening Post* ran a story about the whole thing, headlined "Eleven Wretched Women."

But still, Milliat and women athletes around the world kept fighting, continuing to hold women's games and, slowly but surely, making gains with the Olympics and the IOC. In 1936, Milliat issued an ultimatum: either the Olympics allow women to participate in the "full program" or they needed to make it a male-only event, and she would continue on with her successful women's-only event. She didn't quite get the "full program," but the IOC did finally add a nine-event program, and they acknowledged the records set at the Women's World Games. Nine events. Nine hard-won events. But it was a start.

Milliat died in 1957, living long enough to see women in France win the right to vote in 1944. Her work continued through others. The right for women to participate in sports was officially recognized in 1979 at the Convention on the Elimination of All Forms of Discrimination against Women—six years *after* Billie Jean King's win in the Battle of the Sexes.

It took brave women like Milliat to lay the groundwork for athletes like Billie Jean King to come along and change the norms around women's sports, which in turn spurred on yet more change. The International Working Group on Women & Sport was formed in 1994 at their inaugural world conference. This group also developed the Brighton Declaration, an international treaty whose intent was to provide an equal playing field in the world of sports and physical activity. The following year, the UN organized the Fourth World Conference on Women: Action for Equality, Development and Peace in Beijing, where they released the Beijing Declaration and Platform for Action that for the first time specifically mentioned sports as a tool for women's empowerment and equality.

The first woman was finally elected to the previously all-male IOC executive board in 1990. Then, in 1996, the IOC updated their Olympic Charter so it read:

The role of the IOC is to lead the promotion of Olympism in accordance with the Olympic Charter. For that purpose the IOC . . . strongly encourages, by appropriate means, the promotion of women in sport at all levels and in all structures, particularly in the executive bodies of national and international sports organizations with a view to the strict application of the principle of equality of men and women.

The IOC also held their first World Conference on Women and Sport that year, with these three goals: "1. To create awareness about women's role in sport; 2. To assess the progress made in the area of gender equality in sport; and 3. To define future priority actions to promote women in sport." They made a goal of having 20 percent of leadership roles be filled by women in 2005 (which was later revised to 30 percent—a goal they eventually reached with thirty-six women in leadership positions (out of one hundred) as of 2020. And in 2014, the IOC made the pledge to work toward 50 percent women participants and to add mixed-gender events. The IOC launched the Gender Equality Review Project in 2017.

Despite all these global shifts toward equality in sports, the Olympics didn't allow women to compete in a "full program" until 2012. But at those 2012 Olympic Games, women took home more medals than men for the first time. By 2016, women made up 45 percent of participants. That number is estimated to be 49 percent for the 2020 Tokyo Olympics. The IOC has put into place policies, some symbolic and some not, around gender parity, including equal visibility, requiring that each National Olympic Team have at least one male and one female participant, and encouraging each team to have a male and female flag holder. Tokyo also issued a requirement that for the Paralympics, 40.5 percent of the competitors had to be women. This was after the head of the Tokyo Olympics, a man, had to issue an apology for saying women talked too much in meetings.

So clearly, there is still work to be done.

All these advancements, these hard-fought changes in the world of women's sports are not safe. Title IX continues to be scaled back, which impacts not just sports but also the crisis of sexual assault on college campuses.

Abuse in sports continues to haunt athletes of all ages. We have all seen the devastating, heartbreaking mountain of testimony against USA gymnastics by female gymnasts, telling the story of years and years of abuse being swept under the rug by the federation that should have been protecting them.

WOMEN AND FITNESS

The history of women exer- cising is rife with medi- cal myths, sexism, racism, ableism, and fat phobia. For too long, fitness was the realm of "white men" and was not fit for the "delicate" female constitution. Sweating in public wasn't ladylike, nor were muscles on women. When the first gyms started opening in the 1800s, women weren't welcome, something that didn't change for a long time.

In the 1930s, fitness salons aimed at women started opening their doors, but their focus was on "reducing" (i.e., weight loss) and light exercises (working out for looks as opposed to achievement). These places were often touted as a way for women to improve their sex lives and keep their husbands.

In the '60s and '70s, more women started exercising, but from the comfort of their own homes, as they were still not comfortable doing so in public. Jane Fonda's exercise tapes didn't come out until the '80s.

While we've come a long way, a lot of these issues remain. Recent studies have found that millions fewer women than men take part in exercise and sports, with many of them saying their lack of participation is due to "intimidation" and insecurities around their bodies.

As a society, buff women still get judged and side-eyed. Ads for gyms frequently feature a woman in a sexy pose, and gyms' dress codes are often sexist in nature (ever wonder why the male Peloton instructors aren't wearing skintight bike shorts and crop tops?).

Many of the classes or gyms geared toward women focus on self-defense, with the understanding women are more likely to be attacked or raped, so we better prepare them for such an outcome. How disturbing is that?

Beyond these horrific examples of outright abuse, there continue to be ongoing problems around equal pay for women, promotion, and respect in athletics. The issue of uniforms, for one, remains incredibly controversial. Billie Jean King once said, "Ever since that day when I was 11 years old, and I wasn't allowed in a photo because I wasn't wearing a tennis skirt, I knew that I wanted to change the sport."

Indeed, there is a long history of athletic wear for women being designed primarily for the male gaze, with no functionality in mind, resulting in something highly sexist (and sometimes dangerous) in nature. Perhaps the most obvious example are the swim outfits that women used to wear decades ago, suits that completely covered the woman's body and would have weighed her down terribly. It almost feels like a metaphor. When women pushed against these norms, like changing into pants and bloomers so they could ride bikes, huge outcries ensued.

To this day, this remains a point of contention, one that gained a lot of traction at the 2020 Olympics when each player of Norway's beach handball team was fined €150, or about $175, for "improper clothing" when they wore shorts instead of bikini bottoms during their bronze medal match against Spain. (While the women were required to wear bikini bottoms and midriff-baring tops, the men, meanwhile, were permitted to wear full T-shirts and asked to wear shorts no shorter than ten centimeters above their knees.) The women lost the match but released a statement about how proud they were for taking a stance against what they viewed as ridiculous, sexist rules. They garnered all kinds of support, winning accolades from the pop star Pink and being cheered on by other international teams, who followed suit.

> There is a long history of athletic wear for women being designed primarily for the male gaze.

During this controversy, women around the world shared stories of feeling overly sexualized in their required uniform, embarrassed, and perhaps even turned away from competing. The International Handball Federation finally agreed to revisit the rules in 2021.

And handball was by no means the only sport reckoning with this. The 2020 Olympics marked the first time that women volleyball players could choose among wearing T-shirts, shorts, one-pieces, or bikinis.

The 2020 Olympics also saw a controversy around the organization in charge of international swimming after it rejected the request of a Black female athlete to use Soul Cap, a product designed to offer a larger, silicone cover specifically designed for weaves, locs, braids, hair extensions, and thick, curly hair.

It would appear that official sporting organizations still judge Black women more harshly, marking them out as different and penalizing them for success. Tennis great Serena Williams, a Black woman, wore a full-length black bodysuit for the French Open in 2018; it caused a massive outcry, and her outfit was subsequently banned, despite the French Open's generally open-minded stance on tennis gear.

Indeed, sports in general are still primarily available to able-bodied white people, preferably ones who fit a certain predetermined mold. The Olympics has a long-documented history of transphobia, including a practice called the "nude parade" that began in 1968, in part a response to American discomfort regarding muscular USSR athletes. The public wasn't on board with this, so the IOC pivoted instead to less-than-reliable chromosomal tests.

The organization abolished gender tests in 1999, but in 2011—two years after they required Caster Semenya, a Black woman, to take a sex verification test after she destroyed the 800-meter race at the African Junior Championships—they instituted mandatory tests for high testosterone. (In case you're curious, no, men don't have to take these tests. Furthermore, testosterone has never been scientifically proven to boost athletic performance.)

Trans athletes continue to be discriminated against in these games; it wasn't until 2020 that New Zealand's Laurel Hubbard became the first openly trans athlete to compete in the Olympics.

• • • • •

Despite over a century of work by activists in the sporting world, the consensus still seems to be that women and gender nonconforming athletes are lesser. Secondary. It was only in 2007 that the Wimbledon tournament finally agreed to offer equal pay. Tennis player Venus Williams, who was instrumental in securing this win, said to a room of Wimbledon executives: "Imagine you're a little girl. You're growing up. You practice as hard as you can, with girls, with boys. You have a dream. You fight, you work, you sacrifice to get to this stage. You work as hard as anyone you know. And then you get to this stage, and you're told you're not the same as a boy."

Billie Jean King has echoed this sentiment, saying that as girls and women, "[We] go unnoticed."

Soccer players are fighting the same fight as tennis players when it comes to equal pay. It has been well covered that despite consistently outperforming the US men's soccer team, both athletically and in terms of spectators, the US women's soccer team was engaged in a lengthy battle with their governing organization to fight for equal pay, equipment, and opportunities.

However, some good news! In May 2022, just as we were finishing up this book, the United States Women's National Teams Players Association, the United States National Soccer Team Players Association, and the United States Soccer Federation reached a historic agreement that ensures equal pay for both the women's and men's teams. This agreement stands to truly even out the playing field of not just American soccer but international women's soccer. As part of this agreement, US Soccer became the first federation *ever* to require equal FIFA World Cup prize money for both the women's and men's national teams. That's huge.

> Soccer players are fighting the same fight as tennis players when it comes to equal pay.

The same battle is going on in other sports. In March 2021, at the NCAA basketball tournaments, a set of much-shared photos compared the extensive men's weight-room facilities to the paltry offerings for the women competitors. The ensuing controversy forced the NCAA to publicly own up to the uneven treatment the women athletes faced, admitting the organization had "dropped the ball" and pledged to do better in the future.

• • • • •

It is clear that although women have made great strides in the world of athletics, in the never-ending battle of the sexes we're engaged in with the world at large, it is still a battle. And this battle for increased respect for women continues to be fought, in any number of fields far away from the heights of national and international competitions. The inequities persist in the very language itself. The phrases "hit like a girl," "run like a girl," and "throw like a girl" are still in the process of being reclaimed, often by companies with only profits in mind.

Progress *is* being made, though, thanks to the tireless work of so many amazing women and nonbinary athletes, many of whom may have watched the Battle of the Sexes, who might have heard Bobby Riggs spew his sexist, chauvinistic vitriol and watched in dismay as a lot of the world seemed to nod along with him. They might have watched King say: *No, I'll stand up to this. You're wrong.*

So many incredible women in the world of sports over the years have fought their own battles and in doing so, inspired the next generation of women and nonbinary folks to keep pushing, to keep fighting for equality. These things matter. The fight matters.

journal entry

That girl at the beginning of the chapter could have been me. I grew up playing tennis, and I grew up confident that women could keep up with men, thanks to phenomenal players like Billie Jean King and Serena Williams. These were athletes I looked up to, that my friends looked up to. My roommate in college had a poster of soccer star Mia Hamm pinned to her wall. Another of my friends had a poster of Serena Williams.

That's not to say I didn't feel the same pressures and self-consciousness that little girl did. I wore ill-fitting clothes when I played because I was ashamed of my body. I only enjoyed playing for fun with other girls, because I had convinced myself I wasn't any good.

If I had sat down in front of the Battle of the Sexes, amid all that hype and bombast, and watched Billie Jean King *lose*, I would have been devastated. That type of pressure is not fair—not to players at the highest levels, nor to those aspiring young athletes hoping to achieve their dream. This pressure women face is indicative of systemic inequality issues, the same issues Billie Jean King was so vocal about. The issue has recently come to light even more, in terms of mental health and the particular pressure we place on women athletes. I hate to admit I was part of it, but I was. Had King lost, I would have taken all those feelings of insecurity I already had and internalized them even more.

In my mind, sports have always been a minefield of gender norms and sexism. The male versus female standards of physical achievement. The highly sexualized ads for gyms. The way male sports are advertised more, given better airtime, respected and revered, while female sports are seen as an afterthought, always coming in second (often literally in lineup and definitely in pay).

That's not to mention all the difficulties that haunt young women who are going through puberty while trying to compete. In my middle school, boys would pick a state to call the girls as they ran by, based on how "mountainous" they thought we were, a sort of juvenile version of "locker room talk." The accompanying shame deterred me for sure, and I'm certain it did for other girls like me. I knew I was being judged for my appearance, not my athletic ability. It was demoralizing and yet another of the countless examples of women being reduced to a mere body for the male gaze. Those were the moments when I felt like I counted for nothing more. Not a body that could break records or win medals. Not a strong body. Just a body I wished people would stop looking at, a body that was garnering me unwelcomed and dangerous attention.

That's one reason physically improving myself or going to gyms can be so fraught, for me and for so many others. I want to challenge myself and compete with myself. I like feeling strong and healthy. I like fitting into my clothes and feeling like I look good. But it's hard to separate what I want for myself, truly, and what I'm doing for the male gaze, in that endless pursuit of the traditionally desirable female body. It's a strange juxtaposition of wanting to be physically desired, but not wanting to be *just* that.

The problems we could have discussed here in this chapter that affect us regular women, not superstar athletes—are too numerous to name: body-shaming women at the gym, the rise of women-only gyms, the enforcement of dress codes for women at the gym. One of my favorites: the offering of unsolicited advice. As a woman who has run for over a decade, who has completed a bunch of half marathons and one full marathon, I was once given advice by a man who had never finished a 5K. He was a font of superficial, unearned wisdom. He had tips about my pronation (basically about how my foot rolls as I run), my shoe size, and plenty of pre- and postrace nutrition advice. He offered me a multitude of running app suggestions and shared all his own plans for training, which he then encouraged me to get on board with. I will never forget the ringing silence after I interrupted his monologue—which is what it was—with one simple question: I asked him if he'd ever run a race. I wasn't being judgmental, truly—I was just curious. If he had this much advice for me, a person he knew to be a longtime long-distance runner, he must be some sort of expert, right? The answer was a confident no but with the quick follow-up of, "But I know what I'm doing." The implication: I didn't. My ten years of competitive running didn't count, apparently. It would've been laughable if it hadn't been so infuriating.

Working out, something that should be about betterment and empowerment and just doing what you want has, for women, like so many other things, gotten all tied up with sexism, patriarchy, and the male gaze. It's everywhere. The entire idea of women working out has long been about being able to attract men or being able to have better sex with them. A thinner, slimmer body for women and a bulkier, more muscular body for men, just like those norms from the first Olympics, which still exist to this day.

There were and are other issues of course, particularly around access. I was an able-bodied white girl from a middle-class family in a rural area, all things that impacted what I could do, and what I thought I could do. Growing up, I participated in volleyball, soccer, basketball, and dance. But gymnastics was my favorite. I loved it; I thought I wanted to be a gymnast. I remember the 1996 Atlanta Olympics so clearly. Although I wasn't at the official event, I watched and rewatched every single event as the American women's gymnastics team became the first to win a gold medal for the country. I was so inspired.

Years later, I quit gymnastics, convinced I couldn't succeed, too afraid of losing, tired of feeling awkward and chubby in my unitard.

Years later, when I learned about Larry Nassar and the abuse he inflicted on the young girls and women on Team USA, I wondered if that could have been my fate. If I had overcome all the self-doubt and pressure I put on myself to make it further in the sport, would the world have found other, far more disturbing ways to let me know I still couldn't compete, that I wasn't enough, that I still was at the mercy of those more powerful than me?

I'm a really competitive person; I might never have been Olympics-level good, but who knows, I could have been pretty good. I hate that I gave up, but I also see why I did. It's hard to blame a mere child for giving up in the face of the messaging from all sides.

Women won't always win these matchups around sexism. To start this chapter, we painted a picture of a girl being turned away from tennis in the face of Billie Jean King's loss. But that girl could have also turned that burning loss into fiery determination to be the one to win the next Battle of the Sexes. We saw a similar thing in the 2016 election when Hillary Clinton, a far more qualified candidate than Donald Trump, lost to that troll and caricature of sexism. While so many of us marginalized folks were demoralized, we picked ourselves up. The 2017 Women's March was the largest single-day protest of all time. More women and nonbinary folks ran for office than ever before. We were fired up. We were furious. We had the feeling that maybe we had lost the battle, but that there were so many more we would need to fight.

I keep coming back to this idea that feminism is inevitable. Even so, we must protect the light of it and never stop working to keep that flame lit every step of the way.

We will never stop fighting for progress. And as we do so, we need to remember each and every accomplishment, honor them, scream joyously about them. We need more moments like Billie Jean King's, triumphing in the face of so much doubt, misogyny, and outright hate. We need to keep celebrating these moments, remember all we have accomplished, and gild those moments of pride with the same fever and fury to fuel our determination to keep pushing for more.

ACTIVITY

```
Q  I  U  V  Q  A  D  W  H  H  N  X  V  D  Z  U  A  G  V  L
K  X  D  K  Z  E  I  G  M  M  S  X  O  X  Q  Y  N  L  L  I
T  W  X  F  B  B  S  T  R  A  F  I  U  O  N  I  R  D  Y  M
I  P  D  A  R  X  D  F  T  E  J  D  N  E  K  B  B  W  Q  S
N  I  O  H  C  Z  P  R  Y  U  E  O  M  N  B  D  X  E  E  G
O  B  Q  V  G  B  H  Q  W  J  J  E  A  G  E  P  M  X  Z  Y
D  L  N  E  C  S  Q  X  M  H  S  E  I  S  R  T  E  B  V  Q
E  R  M  N  Q  K  C  A  X  R  J  E  C  G  J  S  A  F  S  B
L  H  Z  U  V  T  Q  M  E  E  Z  I  R  B  E  D  D  S  T  L
B  X  I  S  U  Y  L  T  I  I  P  A  H  H  W  I  H  H  H  E
M  I  G  W  H  S  S  L  R  M  N  B  T  Y  B  F  N  N  A  N
I  E  Z  I  I  A  L  P  Y  D  B  F  S  K  Q  M  U  B  T  A
W  L  E  L  C  I  D  L  S  I  O  T  T  H  X  U  H  U  G  O
T  T  I  L  B  P  O  L  L  E  Z  C  X  B  K  I  R  Y  E  M
J  I  K  I  K  T  A  I  L  L  I  M  E  C  I  L  A  P  L  I
M  T  L  A  O  M  A  T  B  N  N  Y  M  I  A  H  A  M  M  O
Q  O  M  M  X  K  T  X  M  X  T  A  Q  D  W  Z  V  S  G  S
Y  H  R  S  M  A  I  L  L  I  W  A  N  E  R  E  S  L  B  A
C  G  J  P  B  K  N  X  S  L  J  G  W  N  G  X  H  P  E  K
E  X  T  A  I  A  O  M  Q  Q  Q  G  H  T  W  Y  B  X  N  A
```

TENNIS	BATTLEOFTHESEXES
WIMBLEDON	OLYMPICS
BILLIEJEANKING	ALICEMILLIAT
VENUSWILLIAMS	MIAHAMM
SERENAWILLIAMS	CASTERSEMENYA
TITLEIX	NAOMIOSAKA
GRANDSLAM	

< WOMEN MAKING MOVES PRESENTS >

THE CIVIL RIGHTS MOVEMENT

SMNTY WARNING

If they don't give you a seat at the table, bring a folding chair.
—SHIRLEY CHISHOLM

- Brief mention of racial/ hate crimes.
- Racial trauma.

THE WOMEN BEHIND
THE CIVIL RIGHTS MOVEMENT

Septima Poinsette Clark

Kimberlé Crenshaw

Clara Luper

Jo Ann Robinson

Dr. June Jackson Christmas

Diane Nash

Dr. Pauli Murray

Georgia Gilmore

Gloria Richardson

...A SEAT AT THE TABLE

Don't make me repeat myself. —HISTORY

THAT AMUSING, IF wildly overused, internet meme never fails to make me smile, because I think of it every time I'm pontificating about the history of feminism. Any conversation we have about what feminism looks like today or what it might look like in the future is predicated entirely on what feminism has looked like in the past. So much of the work we are doing now is directly linked to the amazing work of the powerful women who fought for our rights many years ago.

And let's speak plainly: so much of the progress we have made—and continue to make—is built on the backs of the brave and brilliant women who fought in the trenches of the civil rights movement. But so many of their stories remain untold. Why?

For most of human history, a racist patriarchy has worked hard to dismiss and discredit women of color. When it comes to Black and Indigenous women especially, the number of amazing women who aren't credited or seen is overwhelming. More often than not, their achievements and sacrifices are not only ignored but sometimes even stolen.

Our history is rife with ugly moments of not just denying credit to or refusing to celebrate BIPOC (Black and Indigenous people of color) women but often of going one step further—sacrificing them and their stories for the sake of the status quo. Our country has profited off the work of women of color (WOC) for centuries and continues to do so today.

Luckily, plenty of WOC are still fighting to right these wrongs, not just for themselves but for all the marginalized. And we, as a community, must help fight this fight. We, too, are responsible to help ensure we do not forget or slip back into the mistakes of the past by letting the history of these powerful women fade away.

Though we have made some progress, the problem is still far from solved. It seems history is too quick to ignore the amazing things these women have done—and the changes they continue to work toward. So we wanted to take a minute to shine a light on some women whose brave actions and hard work have made indelible changes to our world. These women have been working for decades to iron out some of the systemic inequality we continue to struggle with, while working to strike down some of the most racist policies inherent in our society.

Here are some women you should definitely get to know if you haven't heard of them. Not all these women are people of color, but they have all had a huge impact on the civil rights movement and countless human rights movements since. They are an inspiration to all of us.

First, an introduction to the movement itself. When most of us think about the pivotal moment of the civil rights movement, we think of the Selma to Montgomery March on March 7, 1965, a day that will forever be remembered as Bloody Sunday.

The Selma March, as it was originally intended, was made up of three marches that would take place between Selma and Montgomery, Alabama. It was put together by organizations like the Dallas County Voters League (DCVL), the Student Nonviolent Coordinating Committee (SNCC), and the Southern Christian Leadership Conference (SCLC).

The Selma marches were indeed a turning point in the civil rights and voting rights movement. The peaceful march on March 7 devolved into chaos and rioting. The horrific scenes of violence and continued racism that led to the injury and even death of the protesters shone a massive spotlight on the movement.

But the marchers kept on marching. They marched again on March 9. Although the governor of Alabama refused to commit to protecting the protesters from violence, President Lyndon Johnson was moved to do so. On the third and final protest, on March 21, the protesters were accompanied by the National Guard.

The uproar surrounding this event eventually led to the signing of the Voting Rights Act (VRA) by President Lyndon Johnson in August 1965, which held that state and local governments could not pass laws that denied people the equal right to vote based on their race.

And though we don't have nearly enough space in this chapter to dwell too long on the slow and steady, yet constant, gutting of the VRA, we do think it is important to note that in 2013, the Supreme Court ruling on Shelby County v. Holder, *did just that by further weakening the VRA. The ruling struck down a key provision in the VRA, Section 5, which required states and localities with historical records of discrimination against marginalized voters to get approvals from the federal government before allowing any changes to voting procedures. Since then, many activists have been focused on getting this provision reinstated.*

CIVIL RIGHTS ACTIVISTS TO REMEMBER

Yes, Bloody Sunday was a turning point of the civil rights movement, but there were so many phenomenal organizations, events, and people involved that led up to that groundbreaking moment. They have inspired so many generations of people who have been continuing to work on behalf of civil rights ever since.

We do not have enough space here to try to offer up a full tribute to the countless heroes who worked tirelessly to help the civil rights movement succeed and who helped pave the path for the passage of the Voting Rights Act. Instead, we are going to remind you of a few names you don't hear as often as Martin Luther King Jr.'s or John Lewis's, so that the stories of these individuals are told one more time and their names will live on even longer.

SEPTIMA POINSETTE CLARK
(1898-1987)

Septima Poinsette Clark was an activist from South Carolina who assisted Thurgood Marshall on a 1945 case concerning equal pay for Black teachers. As a teacher and a member of the NAACP, she went beyond the standard curriculum to teach her students about the right to vote and about integrated education systems.

Clark also became director of several different school programs that taught not only reading (as many states used literacy tests to deny Black citizens their vote) and math but also how to register to vote.

DR. PAULI MURRAY
(1910-1985)

Dr. Pauli Murray's impact has been felt throughout history, within not only the civil rights movement but the LGBTQ+ movement as well. Dr. Pauli Murray (they/them) was a lawyer, an Episcopal priest, and an activist and a cofounder of the National Organization of Women. Back in 1944, Dr. Murray was the only woman to enroll at Howard Law School; they went on to graduate at the top of the class. The work they focused on during their studies and after they graduated and became a lawyer would be used as cornerstones for several court doctrines that would challenge many of the most egregiously racist laws on the books, including *Brown v. Board of Education of Topeka* and *Plessy v. Ferguson*, which took on the notion of the "separate but equal" doctrine.

In 1971, their essay "Jane Crow and the Law," coauthored with Mary O. Eastwood, was used by Ruth Bader Ginsburg to successfully argue the point of how sex discrimination applies within the Fourteenth Amendment.

But it wasn't just their incredible work within the Black community that made Dr. Murray an icon but their very public attempts to try to grapple with who they were. In their lifetime, the idea of gender identities varied greatly, and the different terminologies of gender didn't even exist yet. The overall stigma against the LGBTQ+ community back then makes it difficult to know exactly how Dr. Murray would have identified today. (In their earlier works, researchers identified that they would use "he/she personalities" when corresponding with family members, but in later works "she/her/hers" were used.)

We use "they" here out of respect for their work in this area, even though we don't know for sure what they might have preferred. What we do know is that Dr. Murray was on the front lines of dealing with the problem of intersectionality in the women's movement—well before there was a term for it!—and their contributions, without a doubt, changed the course of women's history.

AMELIA BOYNTON ROBINSON
(1911-2015)

Amelia Boynton Robinson became a fixture of the civil rights movement when a photograph of her, taken after she had been beaten unconscious by cops during the Selma March in 1965, rocketed around the world.

But that's not the only reason we are talking about her. Robinson had been working for years before that and would continue to do so for many years to come, and her activism opened up opportunities for so many in her community. In the 1930s, she served on the Dallas County Voters League (DCVL), which worked to help Black voters register. She was one of the "Courageous Eight," who served as a steering committee of sorts. Robinson and her organization invited Martin Luther King Jr. and the Southern Christian Leadership Conference (SCLC) to help with the continued work for voting rights in 1954.

In 1964, Robinson registered as a Democratic candidate for the US Senate and received 10 percent of the votes. She and others, such as Diane Nash, alongside the SNCC and the SCLC, also helped organize the march from Selma to Montgomery, Alabama, the one that would make her famous for all the wrong reasons.

On March 7, 1965, almost six hundred marchers came together to protest and march from Brown Chapel AME Church to the Edmund Pettus Bridge in Selma. It was there that they were attacked by state troopers and other white supremacist counterprotestors, and she was beaten so badly she lost consciousness.

When interviewed by the NAACP magazine *The Crisis*, Boynton Robinson stated: "I saw them as we marched across the bridge, some with gas masks on, clubs and cattle prods in their hands, some on horses. They came from the right, the left, the front and started beating people." When a trooper hit her with a billy club, she said, "I gave him a dirty look, and the second time I was hit at the base of my neck. I fell unconscious. I woke up in the hospital."

The picture of Boynton Robinson's prone body would become a symbol of the tragedy of that day. But it also set into motion the beginning of the outrage that would eventually influence President Lyndon Johnson to sign the Voting Rights Act in 1965.

JO ANN ROBINSON
(1912-1992)

Originally from Georgia, Jo Ann Robinson was an activist who was the spark that set the Montgomery bus boycott in motion. On the day after Rosa Parks's arrest in 1955, Robinson, who had succeeded Mary Fair Burks as the president of the Women's Political Council (WPC), printed out thirty-five thousand handbills to gather support for a massive boycott of the bus system the following Monday.

As a result of the success of this push, the Montgomery Improvement Association was created, and the groundwork was laid for the much larger and longer boycott that would reverberate around the country.

DOROTHY HEIGHT
(1912-2010)

Dorothy Height was given the title the godmother of the civil rights movement. An icon within the movement, Height was a protégé of Mary McLeod Bethune, who had been so active during the suffragette movement. Height was known for organizing many events and protests during the modern civil rights movement, including the 1963 March on Washington. But she also worked to bring awareness to the victimization of women (specifically women of color) in the domestic work field.

Height was one of the first activists to openly acknowledge the intersectional need to advocate for both racial and gender rights, which had until then always been thought of as separate fights. Height argued that Black women couldn't just fight for one without the other.

In the early '60s, Height instituted "Wednesdays in Mississippi," a weekly event that brought together white women and Black women from all over to open up dialogue between groups. She used her skills at communication to teach women activists how to communicate more effectively, both with each other and with the outside world.

MARY FAIR BURKS
(1914-1991)

Mary Fair Burks was a college professor who earned her PhD from Columbia University and did further postgraduate studies at both Harvard and Oxford. Burks created the Women's Political Council (WPC) in 1946. She organized the council after she was arrested due to a traffic dispute with a white woman, realizing that her education had long shielded her from the racism that was prevalent around her. Dr. Burks soon had at least forty women signed up to the council, whose aim was to teach the community about their constitutional rights, as well as walk them through the process of voter registration.

The WPC went on to focus their efforts on three major areas of political action: education, protest of segregated services, and voter registration. By the 1950s, the organization had grown to over three hundred members, all of whom were registered to vote. (This, incidentally, led to one of the largest numbers of African American women being registered to vote in a single town at the time.)

Dr. Burks and the WPC would also eventually help organize the Montgomery bus boycott, which was one of the most successful protests to help light up support for the civil rights movement.

GEORGIA GILMORE
(1920-1990)

Georgia Gilmore was known as a force of nature, not only in stature but in how she advocated for the people she loved. Whether it was standing up for herself, her family, or her friends, she was not one to back down. She was arrested on several occasions, simply for pushing back against the racist white men who would try to bully her or take advantage of her or her community.

When Dr. Martin Luther King went on trial after being arrested for helping to organize the Montgomery bus boycott, Gilmore was one of the many who testified to the abuse and mistreatment she received simply trying to get to and from work, because of the bus segregation laws at the time. Gilmore was tired and ready to fight.

After her testimony, she was fired from her job as a cook for a lunch counter in downtown Montgomery. Instead of accepting another demeaning job, Gilmore was convinced by Dr. King to work for herself and help the movement. So she did just that.

Gilmore created the Club from Nowhere, which brought together people from everywhere to sit at her place and eat her delicious food. The money she brought in through her new business helped her raise funds for the civil rights movement. She fed both the community and the movement with her cooking.

FOOD AND PROTESTS

*Food has long been an inte*gral part of protesting, not just in providing food to those protesting (work historically done almost entirely by women) but in other ways too. For example, protest cookbooks and cookbooks written with intersectionality in mind are meant to educate and inform readers about the important history behind the foods we eat, how to honor those histories, and how to feed those who are fighting in an activist ecosystem. For more information, check out *Savor*, the podcast I do all about the history of food!

Gilmore's Club from Nowhere became a gathering place for both locals sympathetic to the movement and politicians and other famous people who would come together at her place to eat and make plans.

After the court ruled in her favor in *Gilmore v. City of Montgomery* in 1959, forcing Montgomery to integrate its recreational facilities, Gilmore kept on making waves. The next battle was for the desegregation of Montgomery's public parks, in *Gilmore v. City of Montgomery*, take two, in 1974. No surprise: she won again!

GLORIA RICHARDSON
(1922-2021)

Gloria Richardson was a leader from Maryland who not only helped organize sit-ins and protests in her community but also was one of the leaders of the Cambridge Nonviolent Action Committee (CNAC), a group working in Cambridge, MD, to fight against segregation and inequality. She was also on the board of the SNCC.

Though the protests Richardson encouraged were nonviolent, she was a fierce proponent of self-defense and defended the right of members of the Black community to protect themselves when they were experiencing continued violence during these times. She was heavily involved in the protests that lasted from 1961 until 1964, when the Civil Rights Act of 1964 was signed.

During the protests, Richardson and the CNAC met with the then governor, J. Millard Tawes, who asked them to cease protests to come to some sort of consensus. His request was rejected, and in response, the governor declared martial law and sent the National Guard to confront the protesters. Eventually the Kennedy administration would try to get involved as well.

After the protests ended, Richardson stepped down from her position at the CNAC but remained heavily involved in the movement in later years, including being part of the National Council for Negro Women.

CLARA LUPER
(1923-2011)

Clara Luper was an advisor to the NAACP Youth Council in Oklahoma City. During her time in the role, she put on a play with the youth council entitled "Brother President: The Story of Dr. Martin Luther King," which was performed at a national freedom rally in New York City.

CLARA LUPER, TEACHER AND ADVISOR TO THE NAACP YOUTH COUNCIL, OKLAHOMA CITY, 1957.

In 1958, she staged a sit-in at a drugstore in Oklahoma, based on an idea suggested to her by her eight-year-old daughter. (She was one of the first protesters ever to utilize a sit-in for the civil rights movement.)

Luper's nonviolent sit-ins were a major contributor to ending segregation in Oklahoma. She soon became more active on a national level in the fight for civil rights, working with the NAACP and as a participant in the Selma to Montgomery Marches.

As a lifelong teacher, Luper was able to both support and teach her students to advocate and fight for their rights. In 1972, Luper became a candidate for the US Senate for the state of Oklahoma.

DR. JUNE JACKSON CHRISTMAS
(1924-)

Dr. June Jackson Christmas is a psychiatrist who specializes in community health care, specifically for the low-income African American community. She also served as health commissioner for New York and later on became a member of President Jimmy Carter's transition team, as well as an advisor to Governor Mario Cuomo.

Dr. Christmas and her husband used their home as a respite for civil rights workers in the South, including offering mental health care and helping with fundraising. Christmas also fought against housing discrimination in New York and was part of a movement that eventually helped change New York City law.

DIANE NASH
(1938-)

Diane Nash was a cofounder of the Student Nonviolent Coordinating Committee (SNCC), which organized the first lunch-counter sit-ins in Nashville, Tennessee. She was also heavily involved with the Freedom Riders, the civil rights activists who rode buses to protest segregated bus terminals in the South back in 1961. Nash was able to help desegregate one of the first Southern cities through her protests and sit-ins.

Nash co-initiated the Alabama Voting Rights Project and worked with the Selma voting rights movement in the early 1960s, which helped lead to the passage of the Voting Rights Act in 1965. Because of her activism and her leadership, Nash would be arrested on several occasions, including being threatened with two years in jail for "contributing to the delinquency of minors" for teaching nonviolent actions to college students. (She was released after ten days.)

Nash would later go on to help lead the Southern Christian Leadership Conference (SCLC) and was soon making headlines on the national level. She would later be appointed by President John F. Kennedy to the national committee that helped pave the way for the passage of the Civil Rights Act.

Nash continued to work as an activist, advocating for housing rights for low-income communities in the Chicago area. In recent years, she helped raise funds for the autopsy of Rexdale Henry, a Choctaw activist who was found dead under suspicious circumstances while incarcerated.

CLAUDETTE COLVIN
(1939–)

In March 1955, nine months before Rosa Parks was arrested for not complying with the racist rules put in place by the Montgomery bus system, fifteen-year-old Claudette Colvin had been arrested for not complying with them herself.

Seven months after Colvin's arrest, another brave woman, eighteen-year-old Mary Louise Smith, was also arrested after she would not give up her seat to a white person on a bus. Both Colvin and Smith were named as two of the five plaintiffs in the 1956 *Browder v. Gayle* case, which ruled that bus segregation was unconstitutional.

The roots of the boycott can be traced back many years, thanks to the dogged work of the Women's Political Council (WPC), which had been formed nearly a decade earlier, in 1946. The WPC was well aware of the impact of these laws on the domestic workers at the time and had been demanding change since their founding.

Colvin's arrest galvanized the WPC, who started gathering support for a bus boycott with other local organizations and started putting up flyers and organizing meetings. Once Rosa Parks sat down in the whites-only section, the movement had a face, the boycott began, and the rest is history.

Colvin's arrest was not expunged until October 2021, when she was eighty-two years old.

CLAUDETTE COLVIN. A 15-YEAR-OLD-GIRL, ARRESTED FOR REFUSING TO MOVE TO THE BACK OF THE BUS AFTER SHE WAS TOLD SHE WAS SITTING TOO CLOSE TO TWO WHITE GIRLS. MARCH 2, 1955.

MEET THE ARTISTS BEHIND THE MOVEMENTS

 THESE WOMEN HAD a powerful impact on the civil rights movement—and not just to those fighting the fight. They made the struggle more visible to people across the country who might not have been paying enough attention.

BILLIE HOLIDAY (1915-1959)

Billie Holiday was one of the most iconic singers in the jazz world. Scratch that—in the world of music *altogether*. And her legend goes beyond just her talent and her voice; her life was legendary too. Defying the United States government, Holiday dared to sing her music, even after she had been barred from doing so by both the FBI and the Federal Bureau of Narcotics, whose leadership at the time was willing to set her up in order to shut her down. Her song of choice? It's a song that is famous to this day, due to its shocking depiction of the horrors of the lynchings of the Black community during the Jim Crow era.

The lyrics for "Strange Fruit" were originally drawn from a poem (called "Bitter Fruit") by Abel Meeropol (pen name: Lewis Allan) in 1937. He and his wife then turned the poem into a protest song. As it garnered more notice, someone introduced the song to Holiday, who felt a personal connection to the song due to her father's own death after hospitals refused to treat him because of his race.

Holiday first sang the song in a dark room at the end of her show at New York's Cafe Society in 1939, and it caused quite a stir. Her record company, Columbia Records, would not produce it, but she finally managed to get it produced through an independent label, Commodore Records. Many, including some from the Black community, felt it was too controversial to play.

But she sang it anyway, and her mournful voice powers the haunting song that dares to paint a picture of a beautiful day turned into a horrific tragedy. In it, she likened the scent of the strange fruit to sweet magnolias intermingled with the scent of burning flesh.

Her performance of this song never fails to bring out the depth of loss and pain of this era. For so many of us, we know some of the stories, but they are so horrific, so ugly, many people would rather ignore them. But this song will remain, haunting us, reminding us to never forget this harrowing glimpse of the injustices that were swept under the table for so long.

BILLIE HOLIDAY PERFORMING "STRANGE FRUIT" AT CAFE SOCIETY, MARCH 1939.

NINA SIMONE (1933-2003)

Nina Simone was both an activist and a musician. She, much like Holiday, refused to back down. Although she didn't necessarily seek to use her music for the movement at the beginning, she found she could not ignore what was happening to her community as she watched so many of the same injustices continuing to plague the country.

Simone was a woman of talent and anger, a combination that would be considered a threat by many in authority. She used her music as a weapon and became a symbol of "Black rage."

Her anger started early. She began playing music in her church at the age of three. At age twelve, when her parents were moved from their seats to make way for white people at one of her performances, she refused to play until her parents were able to return to those seats.

IMPORTANT FICTIONAL WOMAN ALERT!

The Star Trek character Nyota Uhura, originally played by Nichelle Nichols, was one of the first Black American characters in an integral, nonmenial role in an American television show, which debuted in the '60s. When Nichols was contemplating leaving the role in the late 1960s, Martin Luther King Jr. sat with her and told her, "You cannot do that. . . . For the first time, we are being seen the world over as we should be seen." Nichols passed away during the writing of this book, in July 2022, at the age of eighty-nine. This unforgettable woman had an enormous impact and was an inspiration to so many.

Over time, as she became more active, she came to understand how the system had been created to work against her. She began to speak up about being refused entry to different schools due to her race and how these moments impacted her years later.

Her song "Mississippi Goddam" would become one of her earliest public commentaries on the injustices that were prevalent during the civil rights movement. After the bombing of the 16th Street Baptist Church on September 15, 1963, which killed four young Black girls, and the murder of activist Medgar Evers in Mississippi, Simone would sit and write the iconic song in less than an hour. "It was my first civil rights song, and it erupted out of me quicker than I could write it down," she said.

Her song caused a massive backlash. People sent back records or even just destroyed them. The song was banned in many Southern states in the US. But that didn't stop her from performing it. She would also go on to remake "Strange Fruit," which would become a hit for her as well. For the rest of her career, she continued to use her music as a platform for justice and equality.

WHERE DOES THIS LEAVE US TODAY?

As much as I love reminding people about these inspiring lights of our feminist past, there are other shifts in the stories we tell about the history of feminism—more recent ones—that are vital for us to understand.

One of the biggest historical roadblocks when it comes to feminism and equality is the long-overlooked problem of the intersection of race, gender, sexual orientation, disabilities, and other factors. For so long, intersectionality wasn't even discussed.

One big problem: terminology. In fact, there wasn't even a word for this complexity until, as we mentioned in our introduction, a legal scholar named Kimberlé Crenshaw coined that very term—*intersectionality*—in a 1989 paper.

History shows clearly how important it is to help break down the power structures that continue to oppress the marginalized. A prime example is the suffragette movement, which was white-led and pretty openly opposed to advocating for the Black vote, let alone encouraging any involvement from the women of the Black community. When we examine the beginning of the feminist movement, we can see that it was a play for equality among the white community and no one else.

> History shows clearly how important it is to help break down the power structures that continue to oppress the marginalized.

Crenshaw says she coined this term out of necessity, because she wanted to be able to interconnect those facing oppression from several marginalized communities. She wanted to bring attention to the fact that discrimination can overlap and cause a bigger disparity for some marginalized groups over others.

Although the term existed since 1989, it didn't start to be adopted into feminist objectives until the 2000s. The fact that it took until then for the idea to catch fire is a sign of how far we still have to go in this fight.

Crenshaw, a leader and expert in Black feminist legal theory, has long been researching and writing about the issue of intersectionality and the overall erasure of Black women, specifically when it comes to sexual harassment and abuse. She was on the legal team for Anita Hill during the case against Supreme Court Justice Clarence Thomas in 1991.

When Crenshaw talks about her experience as a lawyer, it is clear she had a front-row seat in seeing the theoretical differences when it came to Black women within the legal profession. What she saw was a broken system that pitted two movements, the feminist movement and the antiracist movement, against each other, leaving Black women as the most vulnerable group for oppression. Crenshaw spoke out on how feminism had long failed to recognize how race plays a key role in making women of color more vulnerable for unequal treatment and more likely to be left behind or out of the narrative of equality altogether.

Within the theory of intersectionality, there is another recently coined term that raises a great deal of controversy as well: *misogynoir*. *Misogynoir* is a word first penned by Dr. Moya Bailey, which describes a specific type of discrimination felt by Black women; in her words, it denotes "the anti-black racist misogyny that black women experience."

Bailey initially used the term in 2010 when she was discussing misogyny toward Black women in hip-hop. The usage of the term has grown more and more widespread as we continue to fight for Black women to be credited for their work, as we battle back against the usage of sexist and racist stereotypes that belittle and dehumanize Black women, not just in the music industry but in society at large.

Crenshaw's work is still considered controversial. So is Bailey's. As debate continues over what is educational and what is mere propaganda, and arguments about subjects like intersectionality and critical race theory cause firestorms around the country, sometimes it feels like we are slipping backward.

As terminology changes and movements shift in focus, it is easier to identify the various disparities that often plague specific marginalized groups, but despite our ability to identify the problems, it is no easier a fight.

The fact that even the conversation about merely trying to find equity has become controversial is, in itself, dispiriting. While we, as a society, are debating what should or could happen in the future, we cannot allow for the diminishing of the hard work and powerful words of those who have done so much and sacrificed so much. We must continue to speak out and fight to ensure everyone in the movement has a seat at the table.

The fight for civil rights has been long, and there are so many other inspiring women we would have loved to name in these pages—women who have been excluded from our history books for so long. But then this one chapter would be an entire book, and it would still be incomplete. We had to start somewhere. Our current battles over curricula and book banning, and which sanitized, whitewashed version of American history we wish to tell, demonstrate why so many have already had their work deleted and marginalized and have had the credit for their achievements stolen. The history of this country is replete with heroes that so many, even today, wish to ignore, replace, deny. Those in power, especially in our chambers of government, are much happier to give credit to men who look like them, rather than the many women and people of color who have fought alongside (or against) the men in the seats of power.

In this chapter, we have tried to outline some small part of the incredible sacrifices and grueling work of some of these brave women over the years, work that paved the way for so many future generations of fighters who continued their work and went on to push the movement forward. And it's not enough, we know. But we have to keep telling their stories, admiring their conviction, celebrating their accomplishments; we must work to ensure that WE always have seats at the table.

CHAPTER 2

THE PANTSUIT REVOLUTION

This is supposed to be the year of the women in the Senate. Let's see how they do. I hope a lot of them lose.

—GEORGE H. W. BUSH, upon being asked when his party might nominate a woman for president

DECEMBER 17, 1969. WASHINGTON DC

HERE, THIS IS FROM ALL OF US!

THIS IS FOR ME?!

OH MY, I THINK I NEED TO SHOW THESE PANTS OFF AT THE NEXT HOUSE MEETING!

YOU HAVE GOT TO!!

A WEEK LATER...

YOU GUYS HAVE TO COME SEE THIS! REPRESENTATIVE REID IS WEARING THE PANTSUIT WE GOT HER!

I WAS TOLD THERE WAS A LADY HERE IN TROUSERS, SO I HAD TO COME OVER AND SEE FOR MYSELF.

WHAT?!

YASSS!

SHE LOOKS SO STUNNING!

WOW!

ALSO WEARING MY PANTS TODAY!

THAT IS A VERY NICE SUIT! YOU SHOULD DEFINITELY WEAR IT MORE OFTEN! I HEAR IT'S VERY IN NOW.

YES, REP. REID!! YOU'VE GOT BEAUTIFUL TASTE!

WONDERFUL!

IT WAS A LAST-MINUTE IDEA THAT I JUST THOUGHT WAS FUN, BUT I DIDN'T WEAR PANTS AGAIN. I DIDN'T WANT TO TAKE AWAY THE FEMININITY OF THE WOMEN IN THE HOUSE— EVEN THOUGH I DO THINK PANTS ARE FEMININE LOOKING.

On Danielle's first day, she is nervous when she walks in, but she is ready to go. It's hard to believe that she's made it this far. Congresswoman Carol Moseley Braun is the first Black woman senator in the country, and Danielle has been along for the ride since the early days of her campaign. Over the weekend, Danielle and some other staffers have helped situate the senator in her new office, so Danielle has already been able to introduce herself to many of her new colleagues—apparently they work weekends? Soon enough, she'll discover that they seem to never leave work.

But that was the weekend, and it was all pretty low-key. Today is the first day of sessions, so the energy in the office is high. Danielle quietly trails Senator Moseley Braun down the hall as she shakes hands and greets her colleagues. But at the door to the Senate Chamber, they are stopped by the doorkeeper, an older gentleman who has been working there for years now.

"I'm sorry, ma'am, but you can't come in."

Moseley Braun responds, confused but polite. "Excuse me? I'm a senator and need to be here for this session."

"I understand, ma'am, but you and your staff aren't in the appropriate attire to be on the floor and will need to change."

Senator Moseley Braun stopped in her tracks with a shocked look on her face. The staff murmured concerned questions at one another as the hallway filled with other senators and aides, piling up behind them. Many of those trying to squeeze by were men in similar attire, none of whom seemed to be concerned with what was happening.

When Moseley Braun asked again what the problem was, the doorkeeper informed her that women were not permitted to wear pants on the floor, that she and her staff were the problem. The senator, confused and annoyed and a bit embarrassed, moved to the side with her staff to discuss how to proceed. After a quick hushed discussion, Senator Moseley Braun decided to stay. She told Danielle and the others that she hadn't brought any other outfit and there was no precedent for this rule—it was mere tradition and weren't traditions just dated suggestions? After an awkward pause, the doorkeeper begrudgingly allowed her in. The judging glances from her male counterparts made it clear that this discussion was far from over. She ignored them and went about her work, but she already knew the male senators would be whispering about her attire in the days and weeks to come.

After the session closed, Moseley Braun returned to her office. All her staffers wanted to know what had happened. *Did anyone say anything? What do we do? How do we move forward? What should we say?*

One of Danielle's colleagues jumped in, reminding them that this issue had been discussed in the past. Didn't they all remember Representative Charlotte Reid? This wasn't the first time a woman had worn pants on the floor of Congress, and if the House could modernize, why not the Senate? In fact, wasn't this a good thing? This was Moseley Braun's chance to move this conversation forward—or better yet, finish it for good. The staffers all agreed that it was long past time to change some archaic ideas that had existed for far too long. Wardrobe requirements, the most onerous of which were aimed strictly at women, seemed designed to further control and undermine the women who had worked so hard to make it to a leadership position in government. And that didn't seem right.

The conversation went on. The recent Clarence Thomas and Anita Hill hearing had inflamed tension between men and women in government positions, with many women asking aloud how long it might take and what other rules they might need to bend before they could feel comfortable in these bastions of male power.

The senator allowed everyone their turn to speak, then asked Danielle to look deeper into the question. Were these antiquated rules truly written down somewhere? As the first Black woman elected to the Senate in the United States, Moseley Braun was no stranger to controversy or being made to feel uncomfortable in rooms filled with white men, but all the senator wanted to do was get down to business.

Danielle stayed late that night and the next, doing her work and drafting a memo to share with the senator. She thought it was long past time to cause a stir—to make some trouble! She had no idea whether the senator would go along, but she took a deep breath and turned in her memo. The next morning, the senator called the staffers together.

Senator Moseley Braun went over the implications of causing such a stir over an outfit. Was it even worth pushing forward with it or should she just let it go? Did it even matter? But in the end, they all agreed: it was time to shake things up.

Let's cause some trouble! For the next session, they all agreed to wear pantsuits, staff and senators alike, to show a united front. The senator reached out to a couple of her colleagues, other female senators who agreed to go along with the plan, because they, too, had been thinking of pushing the issue. Danielle and the other staffers were thrilled. It felt like they had all stayed silent for far too long—it was time for real change.

When the day arrived, all the women in pantsuits, young and old, massed outside Senator Moseley Braun's office, all smiles and laughter. They could sense that this was a big moment, that they were about to make a difference, not just for women in the Senate, but for women in realms of male power everywhere.

They all began the walk together, some of them holding hands or linking elbows, headed to the chamber, talking excitedly. But once they arrived, they were met with a shocking sight. Not only was the doorkeeper standing in front of the chamber's door, arms crossed in front of him, he was accompanied by about twelve male senators. They stood shoulder to shoulder, arms folded, faces serious. One was holding a petition, signed by what looked like every man in the Senate, that put the hated rule down in black and white for the first time: "Women will not wear pants in the Senate chamber."

The men turned, walked into the chamber, and closed the heavy doors firmly behind them.

"Rules are rules," said the doorkeeper, shrugging, and he took up his position in front of the closed doors. The women stood silently, waiting in disbelief for their moment to argue their case. But it never came.

BUT THAT'S NOT
WHAT HAPPENED

That day in the Senate in 1993, those women walked right through that door in what would soon be known as the Pantsuit Revolution. The long-standing tradition—no women in pants—had never been a formal rule, and these brave women finally decided to change that tradition.

Despite the lack of a written rule in the congressional dress code forbidding women from wearing pants, it had long been enforced as an unspoken rule. And it wasn't until Senator Moseley Braun (who at the time didn't know about this silly unspoken rule), Senator Barbara Mikulski, and Senator Nancy Kassebaum decided together to speak out that the issue was brought to everyone's attention.

Women had long been denied access to congressional sessions due to their outfits, and not just when someone dared to wear pants. At one point in time, in fact, the rules of Congress were so stringent that there were provisions about how "frilly" a woman's outfit could be. If the doorkeepers felt that a woman's choice of clothing was not in line with their modesty standards—bare arms, for example—or even if they just didn't like the dress, skirt, shoes, or jewelry a woman was wearing, they could bar that woman from entry. This happened so often, in fact, that a lot of the staffers carried multiple outfits just to appease these all-powerful doorkeepers.

Although the House had already started to allow women to wear a pantsuit instead of a dress or skirt back in the '80s, the Senate (which did not have many women within its ranks) did not acquiesce to this newfangled idea of women being allowed to dress for comfort and convenience. While men were permitted to dress more casually on weekends (khakis and a blazer), the women staff were still expected to wear skirts and dresses.

But things were changing in Congress, little by little. The previous year, 1992, had been deemed the "Year of the Woman" after the November elections had brought several more women into the Senate, where previously, there had only been two women. It was a year that many spent holding their breath, hoping that more and more women would start showing up, become more vocal leaders, and blossom into powerhouses within the feminist movement. Although many, like former president Bush Sr. (as he made clear above) mocked the idea of women being in leadership positions, the Year of the Woman did in fact make a difference.

This wasn't the first time that pants had become such a controversial topic within politics. Several women within the suffragette movement tried using pants as a metaphor of sorts, as they fought for women's voting rights.

Elizabeth Cady Stanton, Amelia Bloomer, and Elizabeth Smith Miller, three prominent women in the movement, are credited with being the first to wear a new style of trouser. In 1851, Miller apparently arrived for a visit with her cousin, Cady Stanton, wearing a daring new outfit. It was described as "Turkish trousers to the ankle with a skirt reaching some four inches below the knee."

FICTIONAL WOMAN SIDENOTE!

In 1993, the hit sci-fi show The X-Files debuted, featuring Gillian Anderson as FBI officer Dana Scully. Scully not only played against type for women—the skeptic to Fox Mulder's believer—but became a queer icon (I, for one, remember being in middle school, very confused as to why I was attracted to both Mulder and Scully). She also became a fashion icon with her pantsuits: shoulder pads and patterned slacks, so-called competencecore.

Some argued that this displayed Scully's need to wear masculine-style clothes to fit into a male-dominated field. As the series went on, though, her clothing choices leaned more traditionally feminine. She would go on to inspire the "Scully Effect," the name for the perceived impact this character had in terms of girls and women pursuing careers in STEM.

Also, fan fiction alert! The X-Files had one of the first large online fan fiction communities, to the extent that, at one point, Scotland Yard decided to investigate it, worrying it might lead to a Heaven's Gate-type situation.

Miller explained that she had had enough of tripping over her long skirt, so she decided to do the unthinkable and lose the shackles of the heavy stifling skirt women usually wore at that time.

Bloomer and Stanton were thrilled with the idea and immediately started planning to make their own versions of what they had already nicknamed "Freedom Dresses." Bloomer was so excited that she published an editorial to praise this new clothing item in April 1851. Soon enough, requests from women around the nation started flooding in, begging for the pattern of these new outfits. In the wake of her editorial, the new garment got a new name; women all over the country were wearing "bloomers."

Of course, it didn't take long before the critics, most of whom were horrified, began to attack and mock this new fashion. The term *bloomerism* was used both to indicate, with some disdain, that women were suddenly wearing trousers for the first time in public, and to imply that any woman who did so was corrupt and deviant. Bloomer wearers were, according to the disapproving men, women who smoked, gambled, drank, and eventually would abandon their families to live this wayward life. This traditionally male clothing item being usurped by women also seemed to imply all the ways in which women were trying to "usurp the rights of man"—for example, the right to vote.

In the face of withering criticism, these brave women were booed at, yelled at, and accused of trying to destroy the traditional family and harm the reputations of their own husbands and families. Eventually the abuse got so bad that even Miller and Stanton, in the hopes of salvaging their momentum toward suffrage, abandoned the bloomers (sometimes referred to as "the short dress"); Stanton told a friend, "Had I counted the cost of the short dress, I would never have put it on."

They had come to believe that the attempt to change fashion norms for women may have harmed their cause more than it helped, once it had become too big a distraction from the real issues they were trying to address. Most of the women in the movement reverted to a more feminine style of attire, in the hopes of attracting less attention, rather than more. They were rebranding themselves as respectable so that they would be taken more seriously and push through the bigger change they were seeking.

It would take well over a century, and many more brave women pushing for change, to get us to that weekend in 1993 when those brazen female senators and their staffs walked into the Senate Chamber wearing pants, refusing to be kept out of the seats of power. In the aftermath of that moment, we have seen the ever-rising power of the pantsuit. It is the de facto power-broker uniform and is worn by powerful women everywhere, from leaders like Hillary Clinton, Nancy Pelosi, and Vice President Kamala Harris to fashion icons and celebrities like the Kardashian sisters, Beyoncé, and Julia Roberts.

There are so many expectations around women's fashion choices that still need to be changed—from uneven enforcement of dress codes in schools to rampant victim blaming for women's clothing choices (*What did she think was going to happen, wearing a skirt like that?!*). But the Pantsuit Rebellion brought widespread awareness to the uneven standards placed on women not only in Congress but beyond.

And though being allowed to wear pantsuits in Congress may seem trivial to some, the bigger issue at hand is what remained unsaid during this controversy: that rules about pants were being used as a way of silencing women and diminishing the seriousness and legitimacy of women in power. By criticizing and policing the way a woman is permitted to dress, those in charge undermined the work these women were doing.

History is filled with the subtle and not-so-subtle ways men have banned women from positions of authority or attempted to marginalize their presence in the room once they've finally been allowed in. The patriarchy has made clear that it will take whatever opportunity it can to quash the accrual of female power, in whatever way it can.

And, yes, there is progress, but as always, it is slow and often halting. In 2020, we had the largest number of women in history elected to Congress. But even so, there are seventeen states in the US that have never elected a woman as their representative in government. We have had many firsts, though, including the first Native woman to be appointed as cabinet secretary (Secretary Deb Haaland of the Department of the Interior), the first openly gay person elected to the Senate (Senator Tammy Baldwin from Wisconsin), and of course, the first woman (and woman of color) to be vice president (Kamala Harris), among many others. And

WOMEN AND FASHION

*Throughout history, wom-*en's fashion has rarely had to do with comfort or practicality. Instead, it has often been about: (1) hiding feminine bodies and teaching shame, (2) showcasing feminine features for the male gaze, (3) marketing to sell women more stuff.

For instance, women started wearing bras and shaving because of popular fashion trends, primarily when thin silks came into style in the 1920s. Don't even get me started on the uproar the short bob hairstyle caused in the United States during this decade.

Not only that, but history is riddled with examples of women's fashion that were outright dangerous. Makeup and fabrics made with arsenic, deadly nightshade eye drops, harmful skin-lightening treatments, hoop skirts that got caught in the wind or lit on fire. Oscar Wilde's two half sisters died when their skirts caught on fire—this is not a joke! There were "hobble skirts"—skirts so narrow, women couldn't take a full stride—which were designed to literally slow women down. There were unwieldy, weighted sports uniforms. At one point, women wore weighted bathing suits— WEIGHTED BATHING SUITS! (Okay, they were lightly weighted, so the heavy skirts wouldn't float, but still, it sounds like a murder weapon, doesn't it?)

These fashion woes still hound us to this day. Within the past few years, a discussion of why clothes marketed to girls and women tend not to have real pockets went viral. (God knows I always want more pockets!)

And as we saw in the previous chapter, women athletes are still fighting for less sexualized uniforms. Women are still judged more harshly for what they wear, what their tattoos look like, what hairstyles they choose—the list is endless. We've come a long way, but men still seem to think they're in charge of policing how we look.

I'm proud and grateful and all of the things, I swear it. But sometimes I pause and think—it's 2022, y'all. Weren't we supposed to be jetting around in flying cars by now? And yet we still haven't had a female president in this country? There are so many important roles that have yet to be filled by women—we will just have to wait a little longer. Nevertheless, damn it, we will persist.

journal entry

Did you know that in 2017, the women of the House decided to rebel against some of the other dress codes they felt were unfair, such as the rules against wearing open-toed shoes or a sleeveless top. They put out word that it would be #sleevelessfriday, and at least twenty-five women showed up in sleeveless attire to protest the old-school rules.

The then Speaker of the House, Paul Ryan, agreed to take a look at the dress code but made sure he avoided any blame for the situation: "This is nothing new and certainly not something that I devised. At the same time, that doesn't mean that enforcement couldn't stand to be a bit modernized." Of course, he also added that people should be in appropriate attire. But as we know, throughout history, it seems that only men get to dictate what is deemed appropriate, and that continues to be true today, whether in schools, workplaces, or even on the damn plane. (Remember the bizarre leggings-on-a-plane scandal of 2017?!)

On social media and in real life, there is constant scrutiny of the idea of what is appropriate, and almost all the judgment is aimed at women. We just keep having to justify our bodies, our lifestyles, and our existence. The patriarchy keeps getting to decide social boundaries and social norms. Who can wear a dress? How short? What color? Requests for "modesty" abound: women shouldn't dress in ways that might distract a man and lead him to behave badly, right? We have been told that women flaunting their bodies can be blamed for the downfall of men; women's clothing has been blamed for anything from bad grades and bad behavior in school to assault and rape. Why, when a woman gets assaulted, is one of the first questions, "What was she wearing?"

For as many steps forward as we have made as a society, there have been just as many setbacks. When we talk about dress codes, we may not always recognize the misogyny that motivates these codes. Perhaps it seems like a small thing but as we look at the people who are most affected by the dress codes, we start to see patterns, whether it's a way of requiring a specific gender to follow more stringent rules—which often makes it more difficult for them to advance in their career or field (see: doorkeepers in Congress)—or a way of labeling certain students as troublemakers due to what they wear. Students can be labeled or targeted for their fashion choice—goth or hip-hop styles, for example, are considered less acceptable to some. Sometimes, the powers that be just use someone's clothes or hairstyle (typically Black hairstyles, perhaps, or clothing styles popularized by hip-hop) as an excuse to hold someone back or prevent them from getting the protection or the justice they deserve.

Both good news and bad news have come from this age of social media and twenty-four-hour online access. The good news is that we are exposed to more looks, styles, and diverse content than ever before. We see boys putting on makeup on YouTube amassing huge followings; we see gender nonconforming individuals lauded for their fashion sense and all kinds of folks breaking new boundaries when it comes to clothing, hair, and makeup. But there's bad news too: There are still gatekeepers, and nowadays, there seem to be so many more of them trying to keep us women in line. Online trolls, commenters, and fans have no problem fat-shaming celebrities, influencers, and regular people alike. The unrealistic expectation of looking perfect at all times has skyrocketed. Though many are fighting the good fight, attempting to promote more realistic and relatable content—including the body-positive movement—there is no escaping the constant expectation for us to look a certain, perfect way, an expectation that has been shaped by the male gaze and male rules and regulations for centuries.

No matter how many influencers and experts tell us that it's more important to be healthy and happy, the vast majority of what we see and share tells us otherwise. Beyond that is an even less understood yet far more widespread blindness to the prevalence of ableist narratives, which not only exclude so many but oftentimes just outright denigrate or ignore those in the disabled community. Let's not even start talking about what is available in the world of fashion for those in that community.

And this type of inaccessibility happens in the plus-size community as well. The clothing and fashion industry ignores, abuses, or takes advantage of those who are outside societal expectations. I mean, when Beyoncé first started out, designers were refusing to dress her because she didn't conform to standard industry sizing. Now, of course, they are clamoring to do so, but if you need to actually be Beyoncé in order to live outside our society's accepted body expectations, how can we, the normies, even hope to try?

Recently, we have started to see celebrities and influencers speaking out about how fat phobia and body dysmorphia have become dangerous within our culture. People have become vocal in the fight to shut down the unfortunate kinds of practices that exclude those from the plus-size community, such as labeling anyone who doesn't fit a specific standard of beauty in a derogatory manner. As a result of this increasing awareness, there seems to be more acceptance of the idea that past standards of female beauty are not realistic and oftentimes harmful for so many women.

But still, the gatekeepers of the fashion industry continue to perpetuate the overall sexist agenda by controlling what people wear and how they can wear it. How do we break this down? How do we try to delete years of misogynistic and ableist mindsets so we can start over? How can we stop gendering clothes and stop policing what we think someone is or is not allowed to wear?

How do we build a world in which we all ignore centuries of control, and the attendant judgment, and encourage everyone to feel good, beautiful, comfortable, or maybe just a little bit human for a while?

MAKE YOUR OWN PANTSUIT!

The Avatar

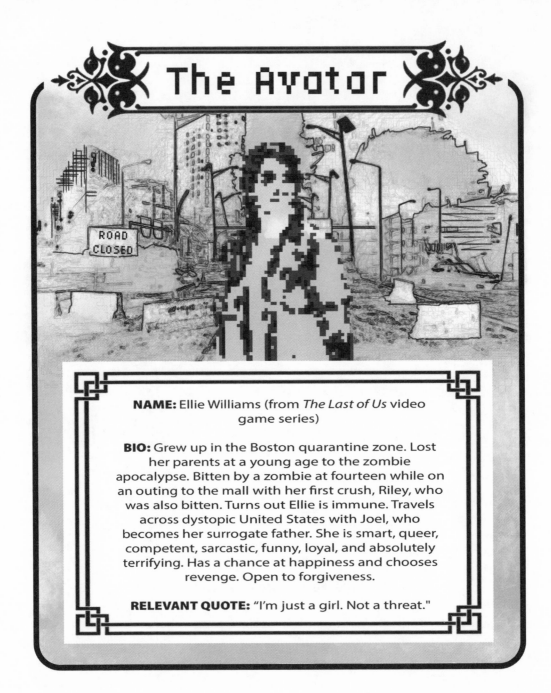

NAME: Ellie Williams (from *The Last of Us* video game series)

BIO: Grew up in the Boston quarantine zone. Lost her parents at a young age to the zombie apocalypse. Bitten by a zombie at fourteen while on an outing to the mall with her first crush, Riley, who was also bitten. Turns out Ellie is immune. Travels across dystopic United States with Joel, who becomes her surrogate father. She is smart, queer, competent, sarcastic, funny, loyal, and absolutely terrifying. Has a chance at happiness and chooses revenge. Open to forgiveness.

RELEVANT QUOTE: "I'm just a girl. Not a threat."

72

BIGGER PICTURE

MORE WOMEN play video games than men. Let me repeat myself. More women play video games than men.[1] And yet, the narrative around it would have you believe that only men play games, that women don't care about video games. Therefore, games are geared mainly toward men. And if women don't really play them anyway, the argument goes, what does it matter if the world of gaming is toxic? Who cares if the few women characters exist mostly for the male gaze and for the male playable character's conquest and storyline? (A playable character, also known as a player character or PC, is a fictional character in gaming whose actions the real-life player controls.) Why shouldn't the female characters usually be skimpily dressed or nude? Don't even get me started on the games that glorify rape.

In over 75 percent of games with only one protagonist, that protagonist is male. Some male video game developers have even stated, out loud, that female characters are too hard to animate. ☹

Video games got caught up in the gendering of toys that occurred in the '80s and '90s, and they were, at the time, labeled for boys. Early video game sellers targeted boys because they wanted boys, rather than girls, as their consumers. The same can be said for action figures and board games, which historically have been highly gendered.

[1] This analysis will of course have its detractors. Often, the statistic differs depending on what counts as a video game, which is a point of contention and, frankly, often pretty sexist. If you include phone games, which are seen as lesser/less serious, women play more. Also, men are more likely to call themselves gamers, though women are playing just as much, according to findings from the Pew Research Center. In 2018, a report came out that made headlines that women had surpassed men in console gaming as well.

The amount of gatekeeping around video games is downright upsetting. The Women's Media Center's Speech Project found that users with female usernames were twenty-five times more likely to be threatened or harassed compared to users with male or gender-neutral usernames. And female video game journalists are two-thirds more likely to be harassed. Perhaps the most famous example is that of GamerGate, when journalist Anita Sarkeesian received sexual assault and death threats for daring to discuss sexist tropes in games. Several of her talks have had to be canceled due to bomb threats. She was sent violent images of herself being murdered or raped by video game characters. Death threats! Tell me again about freedom of speech? Who is being silenced here?

Women make video games, too, despite outrageous obstacles in their way. However, the number of women in the gaming industry is pretty abysmal, and the attrition rate is high. Numerous women have spoken out about the truly misogynistic and toxic work environments that drove them away. As of this writing, one of the biggest gaming companies, Activision Blizzard, is under fire after the California Department of Fair Employment and Housing filed a lawsuit in 2021. The details have been truly horrific, painting a picture of a workplace that was disturbingly hostile to women and other marginalized employees. Stories of sexual assault, misogyny, racism, and homophobia abound. This behavior prevented women from attending work functions and from being promoted, and often led them to leave the company, if not the industry altogether. This has created a vicious cycle where our games are made under the status quo, with women characters as sex objects and women and girl players not prioritized. The potential for so many great games has been lost due to this lack of diversity in the field.

It may not seem like it based on popular news coverage, but video games can have a positive impact on things like brain development, coordination, empathy, and conditions like PTSD (of course, that is highly dependent on which game is being played). Gaming can be fun, rewarding, moving, and in some cases almost life changing. Video games are big business, and they are not going away. And we're telling women and girls they don't belong, that they shouldn't be making them—hell, that they shouldn't even be playing them. And if they do, it's only as long as they obey the rules, don't complain, stay in their (sexualized) lane, as though it's only by the grace of male gatekeepers they are even allowed in the space. Then, the second we raise our hand to point out a problem with the status quo, we are threatened until we leave.

But we're missing out on so much! If we don't work to change the space, to make it less toxic, then it's game over, gamer. Game over.

WHY SHE MATTERS TO ME

I've always loved video games. I think they can be beautiful spaces for storytelling, when the player connects to the playable character in a way that is different from other media. I've played games that have absolutely devastated me, and I've played games that have moved me. To not have a female character in this space that I love, or one that is not sexualized, is equally devastating.

Years ago, I actually stopped playing online games because of the harassment I received. I was twelve at the time. I had a gender-neutral avatar and name, but I guess it wasn't enough. It's strange that as a twelve-year-old, I was receiving countless sexual overtures and threats, yet somehow I just thought . . . *Yeah. That goes with the territory.* Eventually, though, I decided I couldn't hack it, so I had to leave. In my mind, the problem was with *me*.

I kept playing, just not online. A part of me still felt I was weird, that I was somehow trespassing into a world where I was not welcome, and that I was either going to be forced out or hit on because of it. So I mostly kept my gaming a secret.

I was *good*. Not as good as my brothers, I told myself. (*I couldn't possibly be,* I thought.) But I was good. Once in college, I won a *Super Smash Brothers Melee* tournament. I went to a technical school whose population was over 70 percent men, so as you can imagine, this was a big deal. Almost immediately, all the other competitors, all men, ganged up on me, started shouting at me, complaining that I cheated, that I was a lying bitch. I never competed again.

Most of my favorite games involve complex or interesting female characters, usually playable. May I list some of my favorites? Was that a *resounding* yes? Terra and Celes from *Final Fantasy III/VI*; Tifa and Aerith from *Final Fantasy VII*; Yuna, Rikku, and Lulu from *Final Fantasy X*; Claire Redfield from *Resident Evil*; Elizabeth from *Bioshock: Infinite*; Maya from *Parasite Eve*; Alex from *Oxenfree*; FemShep from *Mass Effect*; and of course, that brings us to one of my favorite game series of all time, *The Last of Us*. Marlene, Dina, Yara, Lev, Riley, Abby, and Ellie.

I remember the first time I played *The Last of Us*. When I was introduced to the foul-mouthed, lethal, traumatized, and funny fourteen-year-old Ellie, I felt the strangest sense of relief and bubbling happiness. This game is not happy by any stretch of the imagination, but I was happy to play it and to play her. There were still plenty of tropes, including that of a young girl being the ultimate innocent to drive the violent actions of the main male character—again, find me over drinks and I will discuss them *at length*—but I adored her.

Then [Spoiler Alert: You might want to skip these next few paragraphs if you don't want to get hints about what happens in *The Last of Us*, Part II.] the second one came out and she wasn't the same girl. She'd grown up; she was more cynical. I loved her still, even though it hurt to see—to *play*—the vengeance-obsessed woman she'd become. But seeing her, playing her, you connect. You pour some of yourself into her. You beg her to make different choices. Even though you can't control the plot, like you can to some extent in other games, you control the character and play your part in it, so it feels like a commentary on you. At least, that's what good games *can* do. And the commentary sought to make you question what you yourself have done and glorified as a gamer. The violence, the nameless deaths. It made you question *gaming*, what it is and what it could be, and your part in the whole *thing*.

A lot of people—a lot of them dudes—*hated it*. It's fine not to like something, or to be sad about how it played out, to have criticisms, but a lot of this backlash *wasn't* that. After the new version came out, countless death threats were made to the creators, to the voice actors. The male gamers didn't like these questions. They didn't like being asked to be empathetic, to think about gaming and what's wrong with it. They didn't appreciate playing a woman's violent revenge story, though they had never had any qualms about playing a man's. They felt entitled to a certain type of game. One that didn't put stories about women, queer folks, people of color at the center.

But I *loved* it. I connected to the tale of loss, of choosing vengeance over happiness and the fallout, leading to the realization of Ellie's ultimate fear: being alone. As someone who recently lost someone close to me after our relationship became strained and damaged, who wanted to forgive but couldn't until they were gone, it hit hard. Made me cry like you wouldn't believe. (Unless you're a friend of mine, then you would believe it.)

It's time we asked some more questions about gaming, about why we've allowed it to be so toxic for so long, and what we can do about it, because we have a *lot* of work to do. While we are seeing more games with diverse characters, made by more diverse creators, the backlash is still horrifying. In part because of that, these numbers have actually decreased in recent years. We are going the wrong direction! Maybe if more women join me online, and demand a better world when they get there, we can get things moving in the right direction once and for all.

CHAPTER 3

LGBTQ+ RIGHTS AND THE FIGHT FOR SAME-SEX MARRIAGE

It's our marriage, but not really just our marriage. It's a special moment.

—HELENE FAASEN

- Contains elements of homophobia and violence.

The girl didn't speak to Eva the next day, or the day after. She became despondent, as though someone had died. In some ways, it felt like something in her had. She resigned herself to loneliness, to forever hiding pieces of herself away. Because even when she was around others, she felt alone.

She told no one about the night she'd snuck out to see the first legal same-sex wedding in the world, or the terror she'd felt after it was thwarted by violent protesters. Or how she ran and ran and ran, or how she thought her heart might stop. How she watched the news the next day with tears streaming down her face, listening to the reporter's voice explain why the weddings had never happened, how the couples had been forced to flee before the ceremony could take place. How now, after the terror, these men and women didn't feel safe in their own homes.

The girl didn't understand why people were so furious about love. Wasn't it just love we were talking about here? But the knowledge made her heart skip a beat and her breath quicken. It made her want to scratch at her skin and make herself smaller. Invisible.

The reporter started talking about the weather, like that was the end of the story. It was over. Like the news hadn't destroyed something foundational in the girl, like it hadn't snuffed out the candle flame of hope that she hadn't realized was so precious, at least not until it was gone.

She felt like she was lost at sea without a compass. There was a screaming panic and grief and loneliness inside her that she couldn't even explain to anyone. In that, too, she was alone. She felt like she had died and was now a ghost, watching from a distance as someone else controlled her body.

Eva, who had once brought her so much joy, still made her heart flutter and stomach clench, but it was in different ways, something akin to fear and shame. She averted her eyes when she saw her now, not because of shyness, but because she couldn't bear to be seen for who she truly was.

One night, when the girl was gripped by a sort of self-destructive impulse, she looked up information on Helene Faasen and Anne Marie Thus, the women who would have made history with their marriage, the women the girl had been so excited to see. She couldn't find much of anything. What of their heartbreak? What of their hope?

Though she did her best to ignore it, to crush the part of herself that might make people target her for violence and discrimination, over the ensuing years the girl couldn't help but try to find examples of herself in the media, evidence to legitimize how she felt. She was tired of always questioning and being questioned, of not seeing or hearing about people like herself in the world around her. She had no examples to follow, none that she knew of. Logically, she knew she couldn't be alone. She kept track of all the countries legalizing gay marriage; she knew there were women out there who had gotten married, who hadn't gotten scared away. But it was hard to convince herself of it sometimes.

It wasn't until she went to university and started reading works from gay activists that she allowed herself to daydream again about what it would be like to be fully herself, to be supported and loved completely. To experience that unconditional love she'd been told about and had, at one point, believed she was worthy of. As much as she wanted to believe that she already had it with her family and friends, the fact that she hadn't been completely open with them gnawed at her. Would they still love her if they knew? There was doubt, however small, but it was there. The feeling was devastating when acknowledged and quietly dehumanizing when it wasn't.

Soon enough, she met someone else who made her body tingle and her heart flutter and her face hurt with smiling. Who made her doodle and daydream about weddings again. Who made her consider telling her family. Who made her think that she could have that wedding after all. From their first date, she felt like a neglected flower opening its petals toward the sun.

But picturing their future together, as happy as it made her, was often accompanied by that racing fear she'd felt all those years ago as that brick crashed through that window and those protesters screamed in fury.

Would they ever be able to get married? Could they? After all, they still drew double takes when they held hands or kissed. There was still so much hate. She thought often of the girl she had been that night, dashed hopes, filled with terror, tears falling onto her stuffed bee, the only friend she felt she could be open with. How happy she would have been, how relieved, to know, truly, that someone could love her for who she was. What a balm to the soul it would have been to know that she was not alone. But she was still alone. Nothing had changed. She was still too different to ever find the kind of happiness she hoped for.

BUT THAT'S NOT WHAT HAPPENED

Three years after being set up by friends on a blind date, Helene Faasen and Anne Marie Thus *did* become the first legally married same-sex women couple in the world at midnight on April 1, 2001, the day a marriage equality law went into effect in the Netherlands, the first country in the world to do so.

They were married by the mayor of Amsterdam and were one of four couples that showed up after a call was put out in a gay magazine. All the other couples were male. News outlets waited outside the building during the ceremony, their reports broadcast worldwide. When Faasen and Thus left the building as a married couple, they were met with a wall of reporters. They celebrated with a cake, a champagne toast, and a night hitting up all the gay bars they could in Amsterdam. Finally, at 5:00 a.m., they went back to a hotel room that friends had decorated with rose petals.

A large impetus for them getting married—other than love, of course—revolved around securing parental rights. When Thus gave birth to their first child in 2000, Faasen had no rights to the child because she had no biological connection to the mother and they weren't married. Only a few places allowed for adoption among same-sex couples at the time; indeed, this remains an issue all around the world.

After the Netherlands legalized same-sex marriage, Belgium was the next to follow, in 2003; in the US, Massachusetts became the first state to do so in 2004. The Supreme Court's ruling on *Obergefell v. Hodges*, which legalized same sex marriage at the federal level on June 26, 2015, made the US the seventeenth country in the world in which same sex couples are able to legally marry.

But members of the LGBTQ+ community still face discrimination, both in this country and around the world. As of 2021, only twenty-nine countries allow for same-sex marriage, while three times as many have legislation penalizing same-sex activities between consenting adults, with punishments including, in some cases, the death penalty.

The bad news doesn't stop there. The latest statistics around violence against trans women and, particularly, trans women of color are horrifying. In this country, a slew of laws have been proposed, and some have passed, limiting the rights of trans people. The 2015 United States Transgender Survey found that one in three respondents experienced harassment, including violence, in public spaces based on being transgender (or being perceived as transgender).

There is, needless to say, a painfully long history of discrimination in this arena, and members of the LGBTQ+ community still face discrimination in any number of facets of their lives. Homing in on marriage specifically, activists have been fighting for equal rights for decades, a fight that really picked up in the US in the 1990s. Before that, for centuries, people did their best to skirt the rules: performing a different gender in order to be with the person of their choice, secret marriages, or civil unions or similar arrangements. Oftentimes, being discovered in such an arrangement would result in severe punishment, possibly even death.

Outside of marriage, we've seen discrimination against LGBTQ+ folks at work, at businesses, and in the military. The 1969 Stonewall Riots and resulting gay liberation movement of the '70s, largely spearheaded in the US by Black trans woman Marsha P. Johnson and Latina trans woman Sylvia Rivera, was the culmination of a long history of discrimination and violence against the LGBTQ+ community in the United States.

Johnson and Rivera were the first two trans women to have statues erected in their honor (in the world, New York City claims) in Greenwich Village.

From 1969 to 1974, the number of gay rights organizations across the country skyrocketed from fewer than fifty to more than a thousand. Of note, many activists at the time were more concerned with issues around liberty and individual liberation, sometimes rejecting the institution of marriage as outdated and heterosexist. Some still argue that marriage should not be a key issue when it comes to gay rights, and their arguments have merit. The history and evolution of marriage raises a lot of questions and is tricky at best.

But there is a strong argument for dismantling some of the harmful patriarchal leftovers in the institution of marriage in order to offer a more diverse representation of what relationships, including marriage, can look like. The fact remains, though, that

> The history and evolution of marriage raises a lot of questions and is tricky at best.

in the US, denying people the right to marry also bars them from accessing over eleven hundred rights and responsibilities legally granted by that institution. It is also true that through our media, we have long conditioned young people to believe that success and happiness are equated with marriage, mostly the heterosexual kind. Young girls learn that they should be fantasizing about their wedding day—what their dress will look like, what kinds of flowers they might carry, what hairstyle they will choose. From a very young age, society is teaching them that marriage—and thus happiness and success—can look only one (cis-hetero) way; in doing so, we erase so much of their potential, so many of their choices. It tells them that there is one right way, and anything they might feel outside that is wrong.

Years before Helene and Anne Marie got married in the Netherlands, the modern-day fight for gay marriage in the US started. In 1993, the Supreme Court of Hawaii decided 3–1 that without a "compelling reason to do so," the state could not ban same-sex marriages. However, before the courts could settle the matter, citizens voted for an amendment to ban same-sex marriages in the state. At the time, not one gay marriage had been performed in Hawaii, but the case nonetheless caught national attention and was the catalyst for over forty states to pass Defense of Marriage Acts (DOMA) over the next decade, defining marriage as a legal union between one man and one woman.

In 1996, President Bill Clinton signed DOMA into law on the federal level. This law made it so that no state had to acknowledge gay marriages in other states, and it denied same-sex couples the federal benefits and protections that were afforded to heterosexual couples. In 1999, the Vermont Supreme Court ruled unanimously in the opposite direction—that gay marriages should receive equal protections, rights, and benefits of hetero marriages. The following year, Vermont became the first state in the US to offer civil unions, which ensured gay marriages were awarded the same protections and rights that hetero marriages did, just under a different name.

In 2003, the Supreme Court decided that sodomy laws were unconstitutional; that same year, the highest court in Massachusetts ruled that the state had no grounds to bar same-sex marriages without offering an alternative like civil unions. This decision opened the door for the first legal gay marriage—as opposed to a civil union—to be performed in the US, when Tanya McCloskey and Marcia Kadish were married in Cambridge, Massachusetts, in 2004.

But of course, there was backlash. By 2010, thirty states had constitutional bans on same-sex marriage. During that time, there were a handful of attempts to authorize a constitutional amendment to ban gay marriage. At the same time, some local legislatures were pushing to allow for same-sex marriage, perhaps most famously in California, when, in 2004, then mayor of San Francisco, Gavin Newsom, mandated that the city must offer marriage licenses to same-sex couples. A month after this order, the California Supreme Court overturned the mandate and voided all the marriages that had taken place. In May 2008, the same Supreme Court reversed laws prohibiting same-sex marriage; between then and November 2008, somewhere around eighteen thousand same-sex couples got married.

Alas, the flip-flopping would continue. That November, 52 percent of California voters approved Proposition 8, illegalizing same-sex marriage in the state. After a roller coaster of several court rulings, Prop 8 was overturned for good in 2012 for its unconstitutionality. Religious and professional organizations also weighed in. In 2013, the Supreme Court ruled that the section of the federal DOMA law defining marriage as between one man and one woman was unconstitutional, granting same-sex couples the same federal rights as heterosexual couples. Several state bans were overturned in its wake, leading up to *Obergefell v. Hodges*, which legalized same-sex marriage on the federal level in 2015.

While government buildings around the world, including the White House, lit up in rainbow colors, many other people and entities who still opposed all same-sex marriages were outraged. In the following years, some county clerks refused to issue marriage licenses to same-sex couples; some were even hailed as heroes for doing so, as were businesses that, for example, refused to bake cakes for gay weddings. The arguments often used are moral in nature, implying that any relationship outside of a cis-hetero one is unnatural, immoral, and, if you are religious, grounds to be sent to hell. Some have even made the argument that disasters like hurricanes are God's way of punishing our society for harboring gay relationships. And with the overturning of *Roe v. Wade*, that victory, that safety, that relief of legalized gay marriage was put in doubt, a vital human right that could be nullified on what feels like a whim. That's heavy stuff.

As of this writing, the federal government still doesn't have a law protecting against discrimination based on sexual orientation or gender identity. Most states don't either. According to reporting by AmericanProgress.org, somewhere between 11 percent and 28 percent of LGB workers in the US reported losing a promotion based on their sexual orientation as of 2016, while 27 percent of transgender people reported being fired, denied a promotion, or simply not hired.

Other studies have found that LGBTQ+ discrimination impacts the ability to secure housing, access education, and participate in public life. Young queer people have reported avoiding sports out of fear of discrimination or violence.

Many who reported this kind of pervasive discrimination also reported that it negatively impacted their mental and physical well-being. They reported taking steps to hide their sexual orientation, from lying about relationships to altering their voice. Gay people of color were even more likely to take these steps. Many LGBTQ+ people reported avoiding medical visits due to past discrimination or fear, which directly impacts their physical health.

Historically, we can find this type of health discrimination everywhere. During the beginning of the devastating AIDS epidemic in this country, the disease was often derided or dismissed as impacting only gay men and was therefore not worthy of our attention; there was an implication that it "served them right." We're seeing a similar conversation and misinformation around the monkeypox outbreak in the summer of 2022. All this intersects, because the cost of and the ability to obtain health insurance factor into the matter as well. These factors, in turn, also are directly impacted by the ability to get and hold a job, as

FIGHTING FOR
THEIR LIVES

 Members of the trans com- munity are fighters, whether they want to be or not. They still have to fight to just exist and be. Whether it's the simple right to be referred to in their preferred gender, or to get an identification card with their new names, or simply to be seen as the person they have always felt themselves to be, they fight.

And we, as allies, cannot ignore it when we see injustice. The year 2021 was one of the most violent years in the trans community. At least fifty trans or nonbinary people were killed in this country, and that number is most likely misleadingly low, as many of the deaths of transgender people are underreported, either by misidentification or by deadnaming them, meaning using their name from before their transition, without their consent.

Anti-trans rhetoric within the political sphere has only made things worse. The year has also been one of the worst for transgender rights. At least eight states are ready to move forward with anti-trans bills and laws, with twenty-five different anti-LGBTQ+ laws enacted, thirteen of which are anti-trans. Several of the bills specifically include prohibiting health care for trans youths. Thirty states have enacted different restrictions against trans athletes.

Some states, like South Dakota, have even proposed allowing students to sue if they were to "encounter trans students" in certain settings, such as "if a teacher permits trans students to use single-sex bathrooms that align with their gender identity." This law is engineered to be similar to the Texas abortion law, SB 8, which would essentially allow a type of bounty to be awarded to those who act against trans students.

Of course, on a federal level these laws are dangerous in so many ways. But on a personal level, it is beyond devastating. In 2021, calls absolutely flooded trans helplines, far surpassing the number from previous years. According to one survey, one in four trans youths attempted suicide in 2021.

We have to do more. One possible way to help: working to finally get the Equal Rights Amendment (ERA) signed into law. The ERA, which we'll discuss again in a later chapter, would put protections in place, both for women and for those in marginalized communities, including the LGBTQ+ community. The ERA, if passed, would protect people on the federal level from facing discrimination based on sexual orientation or gender identity.

There is now enough support from the different states around the country, but there has long been another roadblock to the ERA's passage. When it was first being introduced in 1972, the bill had a seven-year time limit. Unfortunately, the final count fell three states short of the required thirty-eight states needed for ratification, and the extension that was requested at the time was denied.

In January 2021, the ERA was again jointly presented by both houses of Congress to be placed in the Constitution; by all accounts, it should have been implemented, but, alas, the right of women and marginalized folks to be treated equally is apparently not so simple. The bill is still hanging in the balance, although President Joe Biden has released a statement in support, and a majority of Americans support the amendment. Some states still refuse to ratify an act that says simply that we all are deserving of equal rights, and equal respect.

This new amendment could make protecting the overall basic humanity of various communities more concrete and stable. But as we know, laws and bills can be overturned or reinstated. Despite big talk at the federal level, especially when it comes to women, and the LGBTQ+ and marginalized communities, we must pay attention to what is happening at the state levels. As we have seen lately, especially when it comes to abortion laws, rights we have previously held as inalienable can be stripped away, piecemeal or all at once. We must be vigilant in holding on to our rights, even as we continue to fight for more and better protection from discrimination and prejudice.

well as to secure a promotion. LGBTQ+ folks have historically experienced documented discrimination in all these areas.

The slew of legislation around limiting the rights of trans people in public spaces—the so-called bathroom bills and the like, which are aimed at preventing trans people from using bathrooms or locker rooms that match their gender identity and are often targeted at young folks in particular—is just the latest battlefront for LGBTQ+ rights. Once again, the rhetoric frequently implies that a trans person is a sexual deviant, a pedophile, or a cheat—or all the above. There is so much toxic, problematic stuff in that one argument, an argument that hinges on rape culture and the sexualization of girls, but the argument offers no solution. Instead it's used merely as yet more ammunition to target marginalized folks. This latest, but no less contentious, dispute is as destructive and dangerous as the early same-sex marriage battles, just an ignorant justification for violence and hate and discrimination.

Shortly before we finished writing this book, another wave of anti-LGBTQ+ legislation swept the country. As of May 2022, 320 anti-LGBTQ+ bills have been introduced in the US, compared to just 41 in all of 2018. There's the so-called Don't Say Gay bill in Florida, which bans the teaching of anything about sexual orientation and gender identity from kindergarten to third grade. There are a plethora of anti-trans bills, prohibiting trans students from sports.

On top of that are things like the directive issued by Texas governor Greg Abbott ordering authorities to investigate parents who sanction gender-affirming health care for their children, an unprecedented legal action largely opposed by medical professionals. Governor Abbott went as far as to label these often lifesaving procedures as child abuse. This opened the door for many other states to follow suit, including Alabama, where legislators recently signed a bill criminalizing gender-affirming care. Under this bill, medical practitioners who provide it could be punished with up to ten years in prison. These are just a few heartbreaking examples.

All the talk of the backlash resulting from the Supreme Court overthrowing *Roe v. Wade* led to a huge amount of instability for gay couples who fear, rightfully so, that the legalization of gay marriage will be overturned, rendering their legal status as a family null. All this has led to an increase in hateful homophobic rhetoric and even violence.

There is a bit of a bright spot, though. After *Roe v. Wade* was officially overturned, President Biden signed into law the Respect for Marriage Act in December 2022. This codifies same-sex marriage into federal law by repealing the 1996 Defense of Marriage Act, which explicitly outlawed federal recognition of same-sex marriages. All states will be required to recognize same-sex marriages, regardless of the state they were performed in. It's not perfect, and there is more work to be done, but it is something to combat the onslaught of attacks on the rights of the LGBTQ+ community.

What seems to be a surprising bipartisan effort to protect gay marriage is actually the result of widespread support for the issue across the country. Attitudes around gay marriage have undergone a massive shift. In 1996, when DOMA was signed, Gallup polling found support of same-sex marriages hovering around 27 percent. In June 2022, Gallup reported that 71 percent of Americans were in favor.

This positive shift is a perfect example of why feminism has to be intersectional. *Roe v. Wade* and the right to privacy and choice, a right largely impacting women, has been overturned; we can now see clearly all the threads of how it connects to things like gay marriage and interracial marriage. These issues do not now, nor have they ever, existed in a vacuum.

The media hasn't been much help in this arena either. Representation, and especially thoughtful, meaningful representation, is still extremely lacking and, by some estimates, has decreased from already woeful numbers in recent years. There's an entire trope in television and the movies called "bury your gays," referencing the implied lesser value of queer characters that, not infrequently, results in their death. When you add intersections like race and disability on top of that, the representation can be almost nonexistent.

journal entry

I identify as asexual and biromantic. If you don't know what that means, neither did I for a long time! And I'm not going to lie—it's hard to talk about sometimes because of the (largely conservative) eye-rolling backlash people like me get when we use terms like these. To clarify: asexuality is when someone feels little to no sexual attraction, although it is dependent on a number of factors, like emotional connection. There's a lesser-known position on the romantic spectrum, at least in my experience, regarding the emotional, romantic attraction you might feel to a person. Biromantic means I can be attracted romantically to a person of any gender, though not necessarily physically, sexually attracted.

Regardless of where you sit on the spectrum of sexual orientation, and even though I personally may not want to get married, most of us understand the power of that iconic moment—a fairy-tale wedding like the little girl at the beginning of this chapter was eager to see. Seeing yourself, not feeling alone—representation matters. I understand the pain and hurt of being denied rights, of being discriminated against and having to hide pieces of yourself. Of vital government protection and civil rights being denied to you based on who you are and the gender of the person you choose to spend your life with. Of fighting to remind yourself you are equal and deserving in the face of attitudes and legislation that enshrines laws that repeatedly tell you that you are less than.

When gay marriage was legalized on the federal level in the United States, I was walking home from work, listening to the news. Tears started streaming down my face. I remember smiling a joyous, fragile smile. I understand the power of moments like those too.

I grew up in a small, conservative town. My immediate family was fairly liberal, but even so, as a child I was afraid of what would happen if I came out. I didn't know any (openly) gay people at the time. I didn't see them on television, though I did read about them in fan fiction, a medium many people derided for what they perceived as young women's sexual deviancy. No joke: for some reason, I thought lesbianism was a type of dance and asked my parents about it. I didn't *want* to be gay—I was already imagining friends and family abandoning me, judging me, having to hide it from folks. Even just the *potential* of being gay terrified me. I was already making plans to hide it. This mentality set in very young.

When my friends would talk about crushes they had on boys in school, I'd try to play along, try to act in a way I thought would be perceived as "normal." I'd play it up, too, making crude jokes and letting people assume that I was really raunchy and into sex. But I felt like an outsider, someone masquerading as a person she wasn't. I kept telling myself my sex drive would kick in one day, that I'd meet the right person and everything would click and I wouldn't have to pretend anymore.

I was *desperate* to experience these feelings of sexual attraction, to get on the timeline that my friends were on, the one that led to a husband and kids and cute house by age thirty. In my desperation, I did things I regret now; I agreed to things I didn't want to do. It was a toxic cocktail; I was trying to fit that mold, pantomiming behavior I'd been told was the norm. I was so *afraid* of not fitting that mold, I started feeling like sex was something I *owed* men. These conclusions were second nature to me, to the point that I felt so disconnected from my desires, from my own body, that I didn't even trust *myself* to know what I wanted. It was always about other people, not just the (mostly) men I dated, but even my family. What would they think if I didn't get married? That I was undesirable? Unlovable? To be honest, too often, I was thinking these things as well.

As I got older and learned more about the LGBTQ+ spectrum, it never occurred to me I could be on it, other than possibly being bisexual. I think this was fear based, fear of being discriminated against by straight people in my life for being gay and also by gay people in my life for passing as heterosexual, for not suffering enough. But also, I just didn't see or hear much about the LGBTQ+ community. I didn't know the terminology, and the terms I did know didn't quite fit me.

Once, in high school, I got called to the principal's office after a janitor found me and another female friend asleep, in separate beds, in the health occupations classroom, while we were waiting for the football game to start—we were in the marching band. The janitor had told the principal we were engaged in a sexual relationship, so I had to go in and tell the princi-pal I was not in fact a lesbian and I was not in a relationship with my friend. I was a straight A kid, rarely got in trouble, so this was *dramatic*. It was yet another piece of evidence telling me I couldn't be my true self or else I'd be punished for it.

It wasn't until I got out of college and started working on a feminist podcast that I heard the terms *asexual* and *aromantic* (and all the related terms) and thought . . . *Huh* . . .

The first time I heard the word asexual *was in the 1998 film* Godzilla *where the term is described clinically and scientifically, and one of the characters says, "Where's the fun in that?"*

I hadn't known these terms existed. I didn't know you could have *roman-tic* orientation, as opposed to just sexual. I think a lot of people still don't know this! And because I didn't know it, I'd never considered it, even though it was always there in the back of my brain. My instinct was always that something was wrong with me, not that something was wrong with the "sys-tem" itself. Still, these ideas stuck in my head. I had yet to feel what I had convinced myself I one day would, what I (and society) had convinced me I wanted—what I needed, in order to fit into our world. This word—*asexual*—lodged in the back of my brain and refused to be uprooted.

It took many years, several relationships, a lot of support from my com-munity, and some education before I shone a light on this thought and gave it any real sort of consideration without immediately shying away. I stopped trying to "fix" myself and all the things I thought might be wrong with me—disordered eating and sexual trauma and the damaging religious and conservative messaging I had grown up surrounded by. I finally started to think—yes, there are some issues that I need to work on, but maybe I'd been too focused on them, on something being wrong with me—maybe I was missing something far more important.

Even writing this down, right now, I'm afraid people will dismiss me. That they'll list all kinds of reasons I'm wrong or tell me how sad I must be. That something must be wrong with me. I'm afraid my exes will read this, and they'll be embarrassed or angry, and their friends will be embarrassed and angry for them, like I'm a shameful piece of their past, someone best forgotten. Just recently, I've had two different people tell me that when someone says they're asexual, something is either wrong with them or they're just trying to get out of sex. I'm *literally* still wrestling with the question Haddaway asked all those years ago: What is love?

I'm only now unlearning that romantic love doesn't have to involve sex, that for consent to truly matter, "no" has to be a legitimate option that we all *believe* is open to us when it comes to sex, at any time, always. That we can never want sex, or never want it again, and that's okay. We do not see this narrative in our media, and because of that, because I didn't see myself, because I had no one to learn from, I had always believed that relationships look only this one way. It's not just the media either. I'd wager every woman who has ever attended a family holiday while single has a story about being asked when they're going to settle down and get a boyfriend. For most of my life, I had simply resigned myself to the charade.

We are fed so many messages around women and sex: how the female orgasm is a myth (not true—oh, I can tell you all the many ways that's not true!), how a liberated, empowered woman has sex and a lot of it (maybe—but only if she wants to!), how a woman who doesn't want sex is either tragic or cold or a conservative prude (again, not true!). We learn so many untrue assumptions that complicate the already too-complicated intersections of sexual orientation, gender identity, feminism, love, lust, attraction, the patriarchy, power imbalances, and so on. I want women to have as much good sex as they want! But I also want it to be okay if they don't want to have any at all.

So many beautiful things come with knowing and accepting how I identify. I've met people who identify the same way and I now am a proud member of a small but growing community. I've stopped trying to fix what's "wrong" with me and started looking at things with a brand-new perspective, one that isn't judgmental or harsh, one that doesn't demand that I keep striving for something that isn't me and I'll never reach. For the first time in a long time, I don't feel as if I'm living in a constant state of failure. With just a shift of my mind frame, something that once was an issue is now exciting. It's like I've discovered a new piece of myself, and I get to explore it. Sometimes I feel embarrassed that I'm an adult still figuring herself out, but most of the time, I just feel relieved and grateful for the opportunity to be able to do so.

I'd be lying if I said it was always easy. I still have questions, questions I once wouldn't have even thought to ask. *What might a relationship look like for me? Do I want one?* Relationships can look all kinds of different ways, ones I never knew existed because I had been so strongly conditioned to think there was only one "right way." And I also understand now that things are fluid, and what I want now may be different from what I wanted when I was younger, and what I might want in the future. I'll keep asking questions and staying curious about all the pieces of myself.

When I look back on the young girl I once was, so similar to the girl depicted at the beginning of this chapter, I wish she'd known how much *more* there was. To herself. To the world. To relationships. I wish she knew it was okay to ask questions, okay to say no, okay to be herself. That she didn't owe anyone anything. That nothing was wrong with her. That she wasn't alone.

While self-acceptance is beautiful, it doesn't change systemic biases. Discrimination is still a massive issue, and although we've come a long way, there is a long fight ahead.

But the power of knowing you are not alone is not one to be dismissed.

MY DIARY

My name is:

_____

Today is:

_____

What am I scared of today?

_____

_____

_____

Things I love about myself today:

_____

_____

_____

How will I change the world today?

_____

_____

_____

ACTIVITY

THE FINAL GIRL

NAME: Nonthreatening girl-next-door name, perhaps on the masculine/gender-neutral side.

BIO: Human woman. Typically has brown hair and is white, thin, young. Quiet, "good girl," virginal. Smart, competent, probably has some trauma in her background.

FAMOUS EXAMPLES: Laurie Strode from *Halloween*, Ellen Ripley from *Alien*, Sidney Prescott from *Scream*.

RELEVANT QUOTE: "Aaaaaahhhhhhhh!!!"

BIGGER PICTURE

HORROR STORIES are, at their core, morality tales. The horror genre serves as a mirror of what we, as a society, are afraid of. Of whom we think is worthy of punishing and whom we find worthy of saving. The "Final Girl" is the ultimate example of this. Who is the one the audience can root for, who can be tormented but survive, who is worthy of surviving?

Historically, Final Girls are thin, white, brown-haired, able-bodied girl-next-door types who are not promiscuous (often virginal) and don't really drink or do drugs. Kind, sweet, nice. Sometimes "masculine" in some way, with a gender-neutral haircut and name. They are the target of the (usually) white male villain's rage and anger, as he stalks and terrorizes them with his phallic weapon, culminating in a confrontation between the two after the rest of the characters in their orbit have been picked off one by one.

The trope has evolved over time. When it was first introduced (before the term had been coined), the Final Girl (sometimes dismissively called "Scream Queen," despite the fact that actresses in these movies have spoken about how physically and emotionally demanding these roles are, sometimes even traumatic) spent most of the movie running and screaming, and she was sometimes still saved by a male character, though not always. These sequences of terrorizing the Final Girl were pretty regularly shown from the viewpoint of the killer, demonstrating that as an audience, we were still meant to objectify her, to glorify violence against her.

The next generation of Final Girls were more self-aware, more competent, and more traumatized, confronting the monster head-on and, more often than not, winning. At least, until he is resurrected, and they do the whole thing all over again in the sequel. On top of that, parodies and other forms of entertainment have played on the trope, flipping it on its head or turning it into a plot device.

For our purposes, there are a couple of interesting things at play. One, clearly, is the idea of the "perfect victim," still so frequently weaponized against marginalized folks in our society. *What was she wearing? Well, she's a slut; look at this picture on her Instagram. She was drinking.* We're experts at victim blaming women.

And if you aren't white, the blame game is even more amped up, or the person of color in question is completely

*American film professor Carol Clover first coined the term **Final Girl** in 1992.*

ignored. Characters of color are given very little allowance for "transgressions" and a whole lot less attention and sympathy if something happens to them. This relates to that whole Missing White Woman Syndrome thing. It's a running joke in horror movies that a character of color (often the only one) is the first to go, and if not them, the "slut" is—a.k.a. a woman who has sex. This character often is killed the most graphically, in a way that sexualizes her and the violence against her, in a way that invites the audience to be gleeful about her punishment. (Disturbing side note: studies have shown that the combination of sex and violence makes cis male viewers more accepting of the violence part.)

If horror movies are morality tales—and I firmly believe they are—what does that tell us? We don't value people of color, and we don't value women *unless* they "save" themselves for a man. The man, and her desirability to him, is what gives her value.

All too often, the audience will think, "Serves her right. She shouldn't have done XYZ." Hmm. Sounds an awful lot like rape culture and victim blaming.

I'm not saying I haven't seen horror movies where someone makes a truly *ridiculous* decision. Reminder: it is horror movie writers who are behind this, and it's worth asking whom they usually give this ridiculous decision to. Often very pretty ladies who, I'm willing to bet, in some cases at least, the writers hate because they feel like they can't get them or have been rejected by them.

I know it seems like a stretch, but we've seen enough real world attacks on women by men who are angry at being rejected. On top of that, we have a long history of reinforcing the idea that attractive women cannot be smart. So maybe it isn't such a stretch after all that horror movies love painting the picture of a really pretty, unintelligent victim, then giving her "what she deserves."

I'm going to be honest and tell you I *have* investigated mysterious noises in the night. Yeah, I've been that girl: *Hey, did you hear that? Let me go check the basement . . .* I certainly would like to think that doesn't mean I deserve to die. I get that some of the enjoyment is the building of tension, then releasing it, always leaving us guessing where and when the character's death will occur. Some researchers think that part of the appeal of horror is similar to the appeal of gossip—we watch things like horror and true crime as a way to learn what *not* to do. Still, this feels similar to the messaging that tells women they shouldn't walk home alone at night, or drink alcohol, or wear provocative clothes, and if they do, it's their own fault for whatever happens to them. As a society, we love to focus on what the victim did wrong, instead of addressing the problem that allows for them to be attacked.

Another point of interest here relates to something called benign sexism. Basically, it's just good old-fashioned sexism, but dressed up all nice. The Final Girl is meant to be a sympathetic character, which makes sense. You want the audience rooting for the main character. But

This is why I love fan fiction. Have I told you how much I love fan fiction? In fan fiction, we all are represented.

A lot of this comes back to the age-old dichotomy of the Madonna and the whore —basically your innocent, chaste, morally good mother figure in the Madonna and the corrupt sexual temptress in the whore. In biblical terms, the Virgin Mary versus Eve.

This idea—that women can be only one or the other, that they are either the caregiver or the seducer—is prevalent throughout our media. The Final Girl straddles the line: a virginal young girl on the cusp of sexual maturity, just waiting for a man to have children with.

the fact that it is a Final "Girl"—the poor thing—is where it gets a little messy. She is supposed to be the ultimate sympathetic victim, and I would argue a part of that is that she *is* a woman. She's weaker. She's frail. She needs protecting. She might have kids! She's been through enough trauma, we've had our kicks, now we have to protect her!

The flip side of the Final Girl is the Disposable Woman, a trope where a woman is killed to jumpstart the main male character's storyline. But the idea is the same. She goes down. The audience approves. And then we watch a violent revenge story

unfold in this woman's name, glorifying in it, because this was a *woman* who was *innocent*. That makes the death worse—she couldn't protect herself, and her male "protector" failed. She is often killed by other men who murder her to hurt the male protagonist, as though she is his property they are damaging. Therefore, the vengeful violence that follows is justified. Despite being the catalyst of the story, the disposable woman mostly only serves as a way for us to sympathize with the violence the male protagonist is dishing out.

Interestingly, for a genre where women have historically

been so maltreated and punished, women consume more horror than men. There are many speculations behind why that might be, but one of the big ones is that women are so used to being afraid and dealing with threats in their everyday lives that it is almost a stress reliever to see it on screen. This is kind of odd, since so many horror movies involve gaslighting, but I suppose we relate to that too. Maybe we see this stalking horror and think, *Yes, that's how I feel every time I leave my house.*

Frightening indeed.

WHY SHE MATTERS TO ME

To me, horror movies are a joy. They feel like a release, like a fun roller coaster ride, the building up and then the relaxing of tension in a safe environment. I will admit, though, that I have been known to take measures like unplugging my television and placing a blanket over it after watching something that really scared me. (Yes, I'm aware that this makes no sense to some of you, on multiple levels.)

For reasons beyond me, I bought all these slasher movies when I was nine years old (and yes, that should not have been possible, but it happened). I fell in love with *Scream*'s Final Girl Sidney Prescott because she was self-aware, competent, and funny, and she messed with the killers, bested them, knew "the rules" to surviving a horror movie. The quips, oh the quips!

While there are many problems with the Final Girl trope, especially that question about whom we deem worthy of survival, these movies, and this trope, have always drawn me in, because here was a woman surviving however she could, outsmarting a killer. A woman who had been targeted and traumatized but kept on fighting anyway. I believe most women can relate to that. It's nice to think we could vanquish the foe, the horror stalking us every day.

But then again, the bad guy/villain/killer is always resurrected for the sequel. And the Final Girl is always waiting to come out of the wings to fight him once more.

 Check out the podcast for my thoughts on the metacommentary in Scream 3 *about executive producer Harvey Weinstein—"Scream Queens: Horror Royalty"!*

CHAPTER 4

THE HISTORY OF REPRODUCTIVE RIGHTS

Whatever the exact scope of the coming laws, one result of today's decision is certain: the curtailment of women's rights, and of their status as free and equal citizens.

—dissent by Supreme Court Justices STEPHEN BREYER, SONIA SOTOMAYOR, AND ELENA KAGAN on the *Dobbs v. Jackson* Women's Health Organization decision

SMNTY WARNING

- This chapter will make your blood boil.

- Even as we write this, the facts of this chapter are in flux. As always, the history holds up, but the future is increasingly unknown.

SUMMER OF 1969.

LATER THAT NIGHT...

THE NEXT DAY...

A FEW DAYS LATER...

MARY AND JUDITH MAKE PLANS TO HEAD TO THE CITY OF CHICAGO, A 45-MINUTE RIDE AWAY, TO MEET THE JANES...

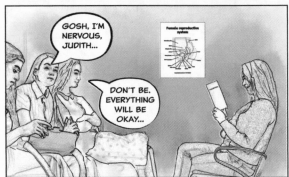

GOSH, I'M NERVOUS, JUDITH...

DON'T BE. EVERYTHING WILL BE OKAY...

HI, MARY. HAVE A SEAT. BEFORE WE BEGIN, I WANT TO WALK YOU THROUGH THIS STEP-BY- STEP. DON'T BE NERVOUS, AND IF YOU HAVE ANY QUESTIONS, PLEASE FEEL FREE TO ASK.

THE LEGENDARY JANES...

As Mary walked through the door of her warm and cozy apartment, she let out a deep sigh of relief. At the sound of the door closing, her roommate, Patty, looked up from her book and smiled.

"Hey, Mary, how was work today?"

"Oh, you know, the same nuttiness that always seems to happen around the full moon, but at least no one got hurt today," Mary replied.

It was true; the hospital had been a little crazy today, but nothing too unusual. But what Patty didn't know, and couldn't know, is that she had finished her shift at the hospital early. But instead of coming home, she'd decided to stop by her other job—her secret job.

A few months earlier, right after she'd graduated from college, Mary had joined the Jane Collective. She knew it was something she had to do, as a way of giving back. After all, the women of the Jane Collective had basically saved her life. And what better way to return the favor than to use her nursing skills to assist other women who needed their help.

After college, she started working toward her nursing degree immediately. But she spent every spare minute she had helping out at the collective. Once Mary finished her degree, she got a job at the hospital but continued her work with the Janes.

It had been years since she'd first heard about the Jane Collective and made that fateful call—it felt like a lifetime ago. But she could also remember that pit of panic in her stomach as if it were yesterday. Her heart still beat faster whenever she thought back on those days.

She had lost so much sleep then, crying herself to sleep every night, sure that her life was over. She was so afraid of how her parents would react, so scared that she was about to lose everything—their respect, her future, everything she had worked so hard toward.

As soon as she'd confirmed her pregnancy at the doctor's office, she panicked. She immediately went to visit a man she'd been told could help her. But as she'd looked around the filthy waiting room, she knew without a doubt that she was in a very wrong and dangerous place. This is exactly the kind of place people whispered about, where women came when they had nowhere else to turn. Then the story would always turn tragic. She wasn't going to be one of those women who died, nameless and alone, from an infection from an unsafe procedure in a sad, dirty room like this, was she? Mary rushed out of that room and never looked back.

It was her sister, Judith, who had told her about the collective. Judith had given her the number to call for that first frightening conversation.

Then Judith had sat next to her and held her hand while Mary called the number and gave the woman at the other end the information she needed. The kind woman told them her name was "Jane." Jane told her that "Big Jane" would call back with detailed instructions. Sure enough, later that day, the phone rang.

"Hello, Mary. I'm Jane. I understand that you may need our services. Can you explain to me a bit about your situation? We just have to make sure we can help you in the best way possible. We need to know a little more about you so that we can keep both you and our people as safe as possible."

After they'd talked more, Jane gave Mary an address.

"Can you get the bus to this address later this week?" Jane asked.

So Mary and Judith had taken the train, then a bus, then a long, chilly walk, but they'd found their way to the nondescript, unmarked building on a quiet side street. Judith stayed by her side the whole time. Ever since that day, they'd remained as close as sisters could be.

Mary would never be able to repay what the Jane Collective had done for her when she was so young and lost. But she knew she wanted to help. In the time since the group's earliest years, some doctors who were allies had trained the Janes to perform the procedures safely so they could protect the women who came to them in such desperation. The group provided counselors for the women and helped raise funds for those who couldn't even afford to go to a back-alley clinic. The Jane Collective did not share the names of the women who came to see them, knowing that one day they might be found out but that these secrets would need to be kept forever.

Mary loved working with the young women who walked through their doors. During her time at the collective, she had started counseling many of the patients herself, sitting with them and giving step-by-step explanations on how the procedures worked, explaining that she too had once been in their seat. She also offered help and advice if they wanted to choose a different path. She saw herself in so many of them, and she couldn't help but remember how it felt to be in their shoes. Meeting her own "Jane," one who had supported her when she felt so lost, had changed her life.

The next day, Mary was at the hospital, several hours into her shift, when the nurses' station started to buzz with news. Some of the women must have heard rumors of her work, despite all her efforts to keep it quiet, because someone pulled her aside and let her know that several of her Jane colleagues had been arrested.

Mary panicked and immediately called some of her collective friends. Sure enough, it was true; an intense fear had already spread through the entire collective. So many women were involved in this underground network, and none of them were safe if the authorities found them.

She soon found out there were other warrants as well. The collective was over, and none of them were safe. A date was set for the trial of the seven who had been arrested. The media had already started calling them "The Abortion Seven."

The news for women would only get worse from here. A few months later, the Supreme Court ruled on a case called *Roe v. Wade*, and to many people's surprise, decided to block access to abortion throughout the land. The women of the Jane Collective would immediately face charges for all their "crimes" over the years. And because of the backlash due to all the coverage of *Roe v. Wade* falling short, these women would be prosecuted to the extreme, with mandatory prison time, held up as examples of immoral, selfish, careless women for others to judge and shame.

Now, when Mary showed up at work at the hospital to whisper with her like-minded friends, they mentioned they were dismayed over the changes they were seeing all around them. Clinics were being shut down everywhere, not just in conservative states but throughout the country. Birth control was being banned in an increasing number of states.

And Mary knew, without a doubt, that countless women were dying in cities and towns all over the United States, from infections or from bleeding out due to at-home or back-alley abortions. All that hope she had, every day when she had showed up at collective headquarters, so eager to see who she might be able to help today, was gone. Those women were all on their own now.

BUT THAT'S NOT WHAT HAPPENED (AT LEAST, NOT IN 1973...)

In 1973, *Roe v. Wade* confirmed that abortion bans were unconstitutional, so the charges against the Janes were dismissed. The Jane Collective, officially known as the Abortion Counseling Service of Women's Liberation, had started a few years earlier, in 1965, in response to the lack of safe abortion access, especially for low-income women.

The women of the collective had been working in the shadows for all those intervening years, helping other women find their way to medical professionals who could help them, when most doctors at the time refused to offer abortions to their patients, no matter the circumstances. The existence of the Janes was an open secret, and news of their services spread by word of mouth. When women called their number, they were told to ask for "Jane," which was considered anonymous enough for them to do their work safely.

But in 1972, two Catholic women had alerted the police, who raided one of the apartments the collective used and arrested seven women who worked for the Janes. The legal strategy their lawyer used was essentially to delay as long as possible, aware that the Supreme Court would be delivering their verdict in *Roe v. Wade* soon enough.

The collective disbanded shortly after *Roe v. Wade* was decided, comforted by the fact abortion had been legalized nationwide. Once the charges had been dropped, the women of the collective went their separate ways. Over the years they were operating, it is estimated that they performed up to eleven thousand abortions, mostly on low-income women who wouldn't have been able to afford any other type of care.

Any of the Janes who are alive today must be disappointed—even devastated—to have lived to see the day that *Roe v. Wade* was overturned. As we were finalizing this chapter, so many of the things we feared as we were researching came true. In June 2022, the Supreme Court ruled on a case called *Dobbs v.*

Jackson Women's Health, deciding that the Constitution did not confer the right to abortion. This decision was not entirely a surprise—a draft of the Dobbs opinion had leaked in May—but was still utterly shocking, overturning precedent by undoing the work of not one but two previous Supreme Court decisions, *Roe v. Wade* and *Planned Parenthood v. Casey*.

As we write these words, this decision—or the undoing of these decisions, depending on how you look at it—is continuing to unleash untold damage on women around the country. Once the decision on Dobbs was handed down, eight different states banned abortion that very day. Several others are hard at work on legislation to do the same, either reinforcing pre-Roe abortion bans that are still on the books or writing new laws to ban abortion in this post-Roe era. Women are still in the fight of our lives, for our very autonomy—it's just that now, the fight has been moved back to state legislatures because we are no longer protected by *Roe v. Wade* at the federal level.

Activists around the nation and the world continue to fight, not just for funding and legal protection but access as well. The battle is raging on, as Planned Parenthoods and other abortion clinics are being shut down in several states and defunded in others. Abortion clinics in states where the procedure is still legal are overrun—but as more states enact draconian restrictions, some women are having to travel farther and farther for health care. This can have devastating consequences—not just emotional but physical. Some of the laws being discussed not only don't have exceptions for rape and incest, but they even protect several fetal abnormalities and ectopic pregnancies, where neither the fetus nor the mother has any chance of survival without proper medical intervention when necessary. These new laws are effectively stripping doctors of their ability to care for their patients properly while also stripping their pregnant patients from their right to decent medical care.

The new "pro-life" narrative, pushed primarily as morality politics in conservative circles, has spread far and wide. It is a very controversial but effective platform, weighing heavily on people's belief systems. And it's making people do crazy things. Do you know there are fake clinics popping up all over the country that call themselves Crisis Pregnancy Centers (CPCs)? These nonprofits often

A WOMAN'S PLACE

It's amazing to think that the passage of *Roe v. Wade* occurred during the sexual revolution, a feminist movement in the '60s and '70s that was simple, though at the time, radical: the idea that women enjoyed sex just as much as men, and that women should have the same sexual liberties as men, and that they should be empowered to express and pursue their sexual needs.

Social conservatives viewed this as an attack on "traditional" family values because women who were perceived to be promiscuous were considered a threat to the family, because women were needed to stay at home and start families and take care of kids and husbands in this very heteronormative and patriarchal understanding of the idea of family.

Many social conservatives blamed the birth control pill, which was first approved by the FDA in 1960, for this movement. The ensuing rise of women in the workforce was another factor that was viewed as messing with this narrow view of a family and women's roles within it.

In a 1968 *Reader's Digest,* author Pearl Buck wrote, "Everyone knows what The Pill is. It is a small object—yet its potential effect upon our society may be even more devastating than the nuclear bomb."

get equipment, like ultrasound machines, via government funding (through educational use disclaimers, for example) and operate under larger religious nonprofit umbrella organizations. They are designed to deceive and manipulate women, pushing them to hold off on any decision about their pregnancy until it is too late for them to choose for themselves whether to carry a fetus to term.

In fact, you are much more likely to have access to a CPC than a Planned Parenthood or any other clinics that are actually medically regulated. That's right, CPCs do not require medical licensure. Although the employees do dress in scrubs and coats, in order to be seen as medical professionals, CPCs usually do not employ anyone in the medical field. Thus far, they have been allowed to operate under First Amendment rights. Although they are offering health-care advice, they are much less likely to be regulated by the government or under the health-care standards than Planned Parenthood and other clinics that offer real medical procedures and expertise.

> As with so many problems in our society, the burden of abortion restrictions falls predominantly on low-income women.

As with so many problems in our society, the burden of abortion restrictions falls predominantly on low-income women. Restrictive abortion laws and outright bans, like the ones we are seeing all over the country, specifically affect those who are marginalized and are already at a higher risk of death, both the parent and fetus.

People everywhere are stepping up—of course we are! Nonprofits have organized to help those who do not have access, by raising funds for women to travel to nearby states with functioning clinics, as well as to help educate those who are seeking help, not only for abortion but even just women's general health and well-being.

But the path ahead has never looked more difficult. Our mothers and grandmothers, who fought for the right to abortion back in 1973, are dismayed that, suddenly, the last fifty years have been erased, and the fight has just started over once more.

The history of reproductive rights didn't start with *Roe v. Wade*, then stop with *Dobbs v. Jackson Women's Health*. There have been plenty more moments of hope (and difficult setbacks) throughout these past few decades. The passage of Title X in 1970, part of President Richard Nixon's Public Health Service Act, was a big win. Title X is a federal grant program designed with the intent of helping low-income families get access to services they might otherwise have to do without, such as family counseling, contraceptives, screenings for breast cancer, testing for STIs, and so much more.

However, the bright spot that was the passage of Title X has dimmed over time. In 2019, the Trump administration implemented what has become known as the gag rule, which effectively dismantled Title X, ensuring that providers could not offer counseling or help with abortion access and services. This new set of restrictions forced clinics and operations like Planned Parenthood out of specific states and areas and cut services from an estimated four million low-income women who depended on these Title X benefits for medical services. Planned Parenthood, who offered services for up to 40 percent of those four million patients, has been specifically targeted for attacks.

Although the Biden-Harris administration did end the gag rule in 2020, centers were still permitted to decide whether to provide counseling for abortion access. And with numerous Republican-led states forcing services like Planned Parenthood to shut down, we are now faced with the possibility of higher maternal death rates, potentially up to a 21 percent increased risk of death. Once again, the group that will disproportionately bear the brunt of this risk will be women of color, particularly low-income women.

These types of restrictions are nothing new and have in fact been used for decades as a way to control women's bodies and choices. The Hyde Amendment is a prime example of these types of tactics that are used to limit access and punish those in lower-income households. The Hyde Amendment was passed in 1976, three years after the passing of *Roe v. Wade*, a response crafted by anti-choice politician Henry J. Hyde to ban the use of federal funding for abortion access and care.

At one time, the only exception for funding was when there was a risk of death or harm—there weren't even any exceptions for victims of rape or incest. With this amendment, the anti-abortion forces stretched their arms as wide as possible, restricting access to

> We are now faced with the possibility of higher maternal death rates potentially up to a 21 percent increased risk of death.

Native American women, federal and state employees, military personnel, and others. Changes continue to be made to the Hyde Amendment, although the news of these modifications is barely covered by the media, because many, if not

WHO OWNS PLEASURE?

Speaking of men reclaiming power over women's bodies, let's talk ... vibrators. Yes, vibrators. Hear me out: we know that women have been using vibrating objects for pleasure since the early 1900s. But still, to this day, somehow the idea of women's sexual pleasure is one we are not entirely comfortable with.

We call vibrators sex toys, marital aids, and novelty items, and there is still quite a bit of shame and embarrassment around this topic. Some states have obscenity laws on the books that prohibit the sale of vibrators completely, though there are of course work-arounds.

As recently as 2019, CES (the Consumer Electronics Show) caused a whole kerfuffle when it rescinded an award granted to the Osé, a hands-free device created by the team at Lora DiCarlo for blended orgasms with women's pleasure in mind. The official reason for rescinding the award? That the object in question was either "obscene, immoral or indecent"—this despite the fact that this same event was displaying VR porn, sex robots, and, of course, the ever-present booth babes.

CES did eventually issue an apology—it was a whole thing—but ultimately, the message was clear: women's sexual pleasure and agency are somehow wrong and shameful, something we shouldn't talk about, whereas men's titillation and sexual enjoyment are nothing to hide or cover up—but should be prioritized and celebrated. Unbelievable!

This history of prioritizing male pleasure and demonizing not only women's pleasure but also our bodies, while

118

simultaneously demanding to retain control over them—as if we are not capable or worthy of doing so—is depressingly pervasive. It imparts the idea to many of us, me included, that sex is for men to enjoy and women to accept in order to do their duty to birth children. The fact that people who can give birth in the US are stocking up on birth control and Plan B in the wake of *Roe v. Wade* being overturned, because we fear it is the next right we may lose, is as telling as it is terrifying.

I had a friend tell me once men don't have to think about the line item called pregnancy that we do, and yet they say we're withholding when we don't want to have sex. They tell us the condom ruins their experience. We take pills instead that can mess with our hormones (don't get me wrong—birth control can be wonderful, but we can't ignore that it can have some really harmful side effects). I had another friend tell me recently she was "closing it all down" (i.e., no sex) until abortion was easily accessible.

So why then is it shameful to turn to vibrators? Sorry, dudes, but they are battery operated and amazing. It's as though sex needs to only happen on their terms, and it's only about them and their pleasure. And to take it one step further, we shouldn't be experiencing pleasure without them. If we orgasm, it has to be thanks to them. And their pleasure is paramount. At the same time, we can't have sex with just anyone—that's just shameful. So take away abortion. Take away birth control. Shame vibrators. Take away any and all control, agency, and independence.

most, people are unaware that such a law even exists. Because yes, it is still in place today.

It is interesting to note, at this very moment in time, as we are mourning the overturning of *Roe v. Wade*, that back when the Jane Collective disbanded, some of the women actually lamented the *Roe v. Wade* decision. Their view was that when the Janes were doing their work, women were helping women, as they should always be, saving them from the tyranny of the principally male medical establishment, and male politicians to boot, making decisions about women's bodies. To them, *Roe v. Wade*, decided based on the argument of a patient's right to privacy, actually served to elevate the concerns of physicians (mostly male) over their female patients. This unwelcome outcome was somewhat of a return to the olden days, in that men were in charge of women's bodies and their health decisions once more. Their concerns seem quite prescient as we write these words, as the powerful anti-abortion movement has recently wrested control over our bodies all over again, deciding that their beliefs are far more important than our rights.

In this tumultuous moment, in the wake of the *Dobbs* decision and a variety of evermore restrictive actions by conservative state governments, the women of the Jane Collective have started to speak up more about their roles back in the day, when simply helping women get access to a safe abortion could result in their own incarceration. They stand by their work, knowing that they took great risks in order to fulfill an urgent need to provide safe, affordable abortions and care for women who needed it. Without them, those women might have gone the route of so many women before them, a so-called back-alley abortion, a terribly unsafe procedure that led to so much anguish, suffering, and even death.

Heather Booth, the founder of the Jane Collective, was unequivocal about what inspired her to work toward her goal of assisting desperate women in need. She had heard about her friend's sister, who was faced with an unwanted pregnancy and had little recourse. She was horrified: "I was told she was nearly suicidal. I viewed it not as breaking the law but as acting on the Golden Rule. Someone was in anguish, and I tried to help her."

And so shall we.

journal entry

June 24, 2022

Today was a bleak day. One that was predicted, but it was still shattering. I've been scrolling through all the headlines, trying to make sense of all the social media panic, but still—the worst has happened: SCOTUS has overturned *Roe v. Wade*. After almost fifty years of constant battling to maintain autonomy over our own bodies, we have been told that the value of our lives is less than the value of someone's moral objections. The patriarchy—and a shocking amount of ignorance about science and the reproductive system—has won today. The anti-abortion crusaders, using the false narrative of being pro-life instead of admitting the truth, that they're pro-birth, have finally used outdated logic and old-school misogyny to take the rights of half the population. I can't help but wonder, where else does this lead?

When the case of *Dobbs v. Jackson Women's Health Organization* was being argued in front of the Supreme Court in 2021, we knew a new chapter of reproductive rights history was being written. Women of the twenty-first century were being tossed into a time machine, sent shooting backward into the past, to the days when so many lost their lives because they didn't have safe access to abortion and reproductive care. I remember those deeply chilling days that followed the 2016 election, when so many of us sat and worried, petrified of what the consequences might be. And here we are.

I can't lie: my heart is heavy. I'm exhausted that we seem to be going in circles. The work of so many earlier activists seems to be coming undone; all I can think is, *How do we change it?* For the last year or so, we have been writing a book hoping to bring some hope and shine a light on those who fought so hard and sacrificed so much to get us to this place, on those who for so long have been ignored or sidelined instead of given the flowers they had earned so long ago. When it came to this chapter, we hesitated on how to do the topic justice. The story of the Jane Collective felt like a spy movie.

THE FEMALE MYSTIQUE

 Speaking of the fight to win back agency! Knowledge is power, and since I've already found an excuse to talk about the magic of vibrators, this feels like an opportune moment to discuss orgasms, doesn't it?? There are *a lot* of myths around the female orgasm. One key point to get out of the way is that, yes, it's a fact: women do orgasm—it's amazing—but I happen to think it's a mistake to make the orgasm the be-all and end-all.

Don't get me wrong; I want everyone who wants to have one in consensual situations to have as many as possible! But I also believe that putting *that* much pressure on having one really makes them harder to achieve. It also

diminishes all the other wonderful intimate experiences we can have—and comes at the cost of perhaps diminishing the situation into just another notch in someone's belt.

It might surprise you to learn that when it comes to women, the very definition of an orgasm is very nebulous and not agreed upon. I'm sure it won't surprise you that women report having fewer orgasms than men (the numbers are particularly low for penis-vagina intercourse). Sometimes it can seem like heterosexual sex is all about men achieving climax and women just going along for the ride.

Historically, society and cultural attitudes toward women's orgasms have fluctuated somewhere between intense interest and pretending as if they didn't exist. The female orgasm has long been misunderstood and a source of repression, shame, and even fear—or the subject of books or pamphlets trying to unlock its mysteries.

In medieval times, it was commonly believed that to have a baby, a woman had to have an orgasm during sex. At the time, scientists thought that women's genitals were just like men's but inverted. In other words, they thought women had to ejaculate/orgasm like men in order for conception to take place.

Unfortunately, some people still use this line of thinking when it comes to sexual assault and rape—that in order to get pregnant, a woman has to orgasm. (Also, if she orgasmed, she must have enjoyed it, so it's not rape.) I'm sure I don't have to tell you that this line of thinking is not just extremely incorrect, it's also damaging, offensive, and dangerous.

To this day, not much research has been done on the female orgasm, which only adds to its very unhelpful mystique. Also not surprising: the amount of research into women's anatomy like the clitoris is absolutely abysmal compared to the amount of research on the penis.

Bottom line: my theory is that sex should be experience oriented, between two (or more!) consenting adults, not goal oriented, with either one or both people hoping to achieve climax at the expense of someone else's enjoyment. Just have a little fun and make each other feel great, no??

The heroism and fierceness in their devotion were something that seemed to be straight out of a Hollywood script, and though they were finally getting the attention they deserved, we wanted to add to the laudatory chorus, hoping that it would just be a part of the cautionary tale of what women were willing to do when people around them were suffering. But the unthinkable has happened—we're back to the days when the Jane Collective first banded together. I can't help but wonder: *Have we failed them?*

Going through the *Dobbs v. Jackson* argument sentence by sentence felt like a stab to the heart. Death by a thousand cuts. I sat there worrying about how this will affect so many other rights that we have fought so hard for since *Roe*. If the anti-abortion movement is truly about saving lives, why aren't they more worried about working to save the lives of those that are already here?

It's even more personal to me. One of the newest additions to the Supreme Court, Justice Amy Coney Barrett, is a vocal proponent of adoption as the solution to unwanted babies—don't abort, adopt! Anti-abortion supporters feel that existing safe haven laws are sufficient to justify states looking to ban abortion; Justice Samuel Alito appears to argue in his opinion that women denied abortion should feel reassured that their baby will find a good home, as the "domestic supply of infants" (a hotly argued phrase that doesn't actually come from Alito's draft decision but in fact from a 2008 CDC report) is woefully low.

Controversy over the phrasing of this sentiment aside, it feels like a slap in the face of those who were adopted (let me raise my hand here), not to mention treading uncomfortably close to the line of what might be considered human trafficking.

I am a transracial adoptee (which is defined as placing a child who is of one race or ethnic group with adoptive parents of another race or ethnic group, according to ChildWelfare.gov) and a social worker, so this argument hit me hard. When we talk about adoption and foster care, it is silly to talk only about the happy parts—*Look, a child is being saved!* The trauma implicit in this complicated path is part of the story too. There are horror stories about the foster care system and just as many stories of adoptions gone wrong. Many countries around the world have either completely outlawed the practice or put strict policies in place, due to the potential of overwhelming trauma and damage to the children involved.

Today, thousands of children remain in foster care until they age out; at no point in this difficult upbringing are they provided the right tools to try to survive the world today—on their eighteenth birthday, they're simply allowed to just walk away. I wanted to believe in this system—who doesn't want to believe that children should be saved and that all children can find a loving home? I wanted to believe in it so much, I chose a career that I thought would allow me to advocate for these children. But when I became a social worker, I found far too many forgotten children who were too often left to fend for themselves, abandoned by the very system that was supposedly saving them.

As an adoptee myself, I had been told I was so lucky—I had been saved through adoption. Any feelings of shame or loss were a betrayal to my adopters; and when it came to my pro-choice stance, I was told that believing in a person's right to choose meant I was betraying those who saved me.

But the truth is, people like Justice Amy Coney Barrett have used my lack of identity and blank past as a weapon against the many who seek to choose for themselves. My adoption has always had a power over me; it strikes me as incredibly unfair that this type of narrative—my story!!—can be weaponized against choice and autonomy. Please understand, I am grateful for the opportunities I have had, and I love the people in my life, but being used as a poster child for an argument I don't agree with is demeaning.

The truth: our welfare system isn't a solution, and it never has been. And to those who pretend that a deeply faulted welfare system like ours is an asset, while at the same time

> If the anti-abortion movement is truly about saving lives, why aren't they more worried about working to save the lives of those that are already here?

advocating for policies that strip as much assistance from the lowest-income folks in our country is an affront to adoptees and advocates within these fields.

I get pretty passionate about this subject. I think many of us get pretty damn passionate about this entire topic! But as we do so, we need to keep some things in mind. This is nothing new. From the beginning of time, misogyny and sexism have been used to strip marginalized people of their autonomy and humanity, so that the powerful can hold on to power. But we have always fought back. These days, we have a better understanding of how to keep fighting, whether it's through political routes or underground networks, so our fight still continues.

There will always be advocates who refuse to stay silent, even at great personal cost. We choose to continue to make good trouble.

CONCLUSION—OR IS IT?

Every time we tried to update this heartbreaking chapter with the latest news, things changed again. At some point, we had to put it to bed. But every day, there seem to be new court cases, new controversies, and new incursions on our human rights. We shouldn't be surprised by now, I suppose.

There are things we can do— lots of things. And we must do them in droves. Any of us who have uteruses know that our bodies are hot topics in morality and politics. Does that statement make sense to you? We see so much heated discourse about personal freedoms and autonomy, yet our very bodies have become a massive platform for political discourse, debated by everyone, not just women or people with uteruses, but everyone else. How did our bodies become public property? Men's bodies haven't. There have been zero public discussions about men's bodies in any form when it comes to policies or laws, or the upholding of past Supreme Court rulings.

It is ironic that, somehow, all those "My Body, My Choice" signs were considered an abomination when women used them to claim the right to decide whether to have an abortion. Yet those signs have quite literally been turned around, the slogan repurposed by the very people that so vilified it, to claim freedom from vaccine mandates in the wake of the devastation of the Covid pandemic.

> How is it that we are living in the 2020s and yet in terms of our rights we have been plunged back into the 1960s?

Rulings such as *Roe v. Wade* stamp into law the right of every individual, as humans, to equal standards, to access of health care, to be protected against abuse and violence. Rulings like *Dobbs v. Jackson* undo those vital rights.

As we have seen, the right to control and protect our own bodies is a slippery slope. The amount of protection the government offers us seems to diminish every year. Somehow the fetuses we carry deserve far more protection than the bodies that shelter them. Once again, this is nothing new. For example, the

Violence Against Women Act, which was signed into law under the Clinton administration in 1993, has expired. As of March 2021, the House has reauthorized the act, but it has yet to be ratified by the Senate. It would appear that, at the highest levels of our government, the idea holds that women's bodies are not worth protecting.

If your blood is boiling right now, it should be. Mine is. Sometimes I feel at an utter loss about what to do about this. How is it that we are living in the 2020s and yet in terms of our rights we have been plunged back into the 1960s, with male doctors and male politicians once again in charge of OUR bodies? We got comfortable, y'all. We thought our rights meant something. We got complacent. One reason we have lost the protection of *Roe v. Wade* is because so very many of us didn't actually believe it could happen. And here we are.

But hope is NOT lost. There are things we can do—lots of things. And we must do them in droves.

THINGS TO DO

- **VOLUNTEER AT YOUR LOCAL CLINIC OR PLANNED PARENTHOOD.**

- **DON'T JUST STOP THERE.** You can also contact your state-level ACLU or Planned Parenthood organization and work to elevate or volunteer with their campaigns.

- **LOOK INTO NATIONWIDE ORGANIZATIONS** like All* Above All that highlight organizations all over the country where you can get more locally involved.

- **PAY ATTENTION TO THE LANDSCAPE—THINGS ARE HAPPENING!** Every time there is a new hearing or policy change, or anything happening on the reproductive rights front that could greatly affect reproductive health care, we need to pay attention! It's not just at the federal level. State and local governments are where most of the action is right now. And local movers and shakers tend to need your help the most, as the national sites are typically better funded than the local- and state-run organizations.

- **USE YOUR VOICE TO SHOW SUPPORT.** Did you know that, statistically, approximately 60 percent of people in the United States support access to abortion? Protest! Speak up! Vote!

- **DID I MENTION VOTE??** Again, it isn't just the federal elections that are important. Our rights are being stripped at the state and local levels. The people we choose to be our representatives at all levels will change the landscape. Those who serve on the Supreme Court and as federal judges are chosen by our representatives, not by us. Every vote counts.

- **EVEN WITH SO MANY STATES INTRODUCING ABORTION BANS,** there are still clinics that provide safe access to women in need of care—we need to support them! The FDA-approved abortion pill is still accessible through the mail (as of now)—we must spread the word and work to find ways to help all women get the medical care they need.

- **NEED THE FACTS ON WHERE TO FIND REPRODUCTIVE HEALTH PROVIDERS?** Go to AbortionFunds.org or BrigidAlliance.org.

129

THE OTHER PILL

*Let's talk about the abor-*tion pill. Did you know that in 2016, the Food and Drug Administration (FDA) approved the mifepristone and misoprostol regimen to end a "pregnancy through 70 days [*sic*] gestation"? Yep, there is a safe way to have a medical abortion without a surgical procedure. Mifepristone is a drug that blocks progesterone, and misoprostol, a medication used to treat ulcers, is used by obstetricians and gynecologists for abortion, medical management for miscarriages, and even for treatment of postpartum hemorrhage.

And on top of that, in December 2021, the FDA approved the regimen through telehealth or through mail order. With so many unable to access clinics due to statewide bans and the closure of clinics, this was huge news! The decision included a statement saying the regimen was noted to be safer than taking Tylenol.

But because we can't have nice things, people and state governments are trying to limit access to this medication. Many states (especially conservative states) are requiring medical officials to be present in order for the medication to be prescribed (no over-the-counter access) or for the prescription to be prescribed only after seeing doctors (not via a telehealth appointment, for example), even though the FDA doesn't require usage to be monitored in these ways. In fact, many countries, such as Mexico, offer these medications over the counter.

Though abortion bans have taken place in many states across the United States, it is a good reminder that options like these are available and accessible (though more difficult in some places) and will help keep many of those seeking abortions safe and healthy. If you need more information on how this regimen works, go check out the abortion pill on FDA.gov or PlannedParenthood.org.

THINGS NOT TO DO

- **DON'T SHARE TOO MUCH OF YOUR LIFE ONLINE.** As different state laws and policies are coming out to strengthen abortion bans around the country, technology and technological companies have become assets for some lawmakers trying to make examples of those who are seeking abortion. We are hearing stories of Facebook (a.k.a. the Metaverse) being used to find evidence to prosecute people who have gotten abortions and those who are assisting them; there are stories in the news about the potential for tech companies to be subpoenaed for private messages, period tracking, or location tracking information that could potentially implicate users in what is now considered a crime.

- **DON'T USE SCARE TACTICS AS A WAY TO BRING AWARENESS.** The old 1970s tactics are not the way for us to protest today. Even with the bans happening around the country, we know there are safe ways to access abortion. To perpetuate old tactics like using the dangerous method of wire hangers for abortions can confuse a lot of those who may feel desperate to find their own solutions. Remember, we have a responsibility to disseminate the truth, not fearmonger; we need to think carefully about the messages we want to send and the best way to communicate them effectively.

- **DON'T USE UNVERIFIED AND UNRELIABLE SOURCES.** As much as we love to see people come together for a cause, remember that good intentions don't necessarily equate with the truth. Make sure to follow verified sources, whether it's to get information about accessing reproductive health care or to find how best to support the fight. As amazing as things like Reddit aunties and viral Facebook rage can be, public websites like these may be misleading. Find sources you truly trust, ones that have been independently verified, and lead others to them.

A TIMELINE OF THE HISTORY OF BIRTH CONTROL AND THE BEGINNING OF PLANNED PARENTHOOD.

ACTIVITY

1870s   Birth control such as condoms, earlier versions of diaphragms and cervical caps available at certain vendors

1873   Anti-obscenity laws, or Comstock laws, enacted, banning dissemination of forms of birth controls

1914   After coining the term *birth control* in an issue of the *Woman Rebel*, Margaret Sanger is indicted for violating the Comstock laws and flees to England

1916   After Sanger returns to the US and faces trial (charges against her are dropped), she opens up the first birth control clinic in America and is again arrested after it is raided by a vice squad

1919   Decision on *People v. Sanger* allows physicians to prescribe birth control to protect overall health of women

1920   The Nineteenth Amendment is ratified

1921   Sanger establishes the American Birth Control League (a predecessor of Planned Parenthood Federation of America)

1930s   Ineffective and dangerous methods of birth control are marketed and sold as feminine hygiene products, including the popular "Lysol douche"

1950s   An estimated $200 million is spent on contraceptives a year in the US, but they are still outlawed in thirty states

1950s   Over two hundred birth control clinics are running in the US thanks to Sanger's continued fight for contraceptives

1954   Trials begin for the pill

1960   FDA approves Enovid as first birth control pill on the market

1962   1.2 million American women are on the pill

1963   2.3 million American women are on the pill

1965 Supreme Court addresses regulation and banning of birth control pill in *Griswold v. Connecticut* and deems it unconstitutional due to a couple's right to privacy

1967 12.5 million women on birth control pill worldwide

1969 Book released on dangers of the pill: *The Doctor's Case Against the Pill* by Barbara Seaman

1972 Supreme Court hands down decision in *Roe v. Wade*, protecting a woman's right to an abortion

1977 Hyde Amendment introduced and passed to ban the usage of federal Medicaid funds for abortions unless the life of the person was endangered due to the pregnancy

1992 *Planned Parenthood v. Casey* is heard before the Supreme Court, which upholds the ruling of *Roe v. Wade* while also modifying some of its original intentions

2016 SCOTUS hears *Whole Woman's Health v. Hellerstedt* and rules that the Texas abortion restrictions at that time were unconstitutional as they would create "undue burden" for women seeking abortions

2018 Mississippi passes the Gestational Act, which bans abortions after the first fifteen weeks of pregnancy with exceptions for medical emergencies or severe abnormality in the fetus, but does not give exceptions for rape or incest

2018 Jackson Women's Health Organization (the only abortion clinic in Mississippi) sues the state to challenge the constitutionality of the Gestational Act, at which time an injunction was granted

2020 Mississippi challenges all the lower courts' decisions and files to be heard by SCOTUS

2021 Oral argument for *Dobbs v. Jackson Women's Health* is heard by SCOTUS

2022 In May, a draft of Justice Samuel Alito's opinion on the *Dobbs v. Jackson* decision is leaked, in which he argues that *Roe v. Wade*'s decision "egregiously wrong from the start"

2022 June 24, SCOTUS decision to overturn *Roe v. Wade* is announced

ACTIVITY

The Villain

NAME: Also commonly known as the witch, the seductress, the siren, the bitch

BIO: The villainous woman has many visages– a spinster, witch, young seductress, creepy little girl with long hair, bitchy boss, ice queen, the evil failing mother or stepmother. Perhaps the thing that unifies these visages most is the idea of "other," of existing outside traditional societal gender stereotypes. And often reveling in it.

RELEVANT QUOTE: Evil cackling

FICTIONAL WOMEN PRESENTS

BIGGER PICTURE

EVERY STORY with a hero needs a villain. There is nothing quite like a good villain; a memorable one lives in our collective minds, is infinitely quotable, and is key in making us believe the hero's journey has stakes that we should care about. They are often the mirror of what the hero could be, were circumstances different, someone or something that we societally agree needs to be defeated, that the hero must triumph over. The villain brings out the best and the worst in the hero, pushing them to their limits, only for the hero to persevere. Generally.

There is no one-size-fits-all villain. Some are truly terrifying, others campy and funny, some a mixture of all the above. Some we can empathize with; some we can't help kind of rooting for. They can make us laugh, make us cry, make us cheer when they are brought to justice, make us question ourselves and all of the systems we live in that could allow

for such a villain to exist in the first place.

One of the unifying traits of villains is that they are outsiders. They are "others," in one way or another. They don't conform to the understood or generally agreed-upon "way things should be." Sometimes, this is clear cut; we as the audience can point to the villain and say, "This is evil," even if we can perhaps understand how the character arrived at their villainous behavior. Others are more blurry, existing in that gray zone, a villain that makes us question the cost of conformity in the first place.

Just as in the horror genre, a villain frequently represents something as a society we are uncomfortable with or worse, something we fear. This means that historically, many villains have racist, ableist, homophobic, and sexist attributes imbued within them. How many villains are scarred, or are struggling with mental illness, or are traumatized, or are queer coded,

or are, in the Western context, distinctly "foreign"?

When it comes to women villains, there are quite a few things we, as a society, fear in women. This is the kind of behavior we view as aberrant and outside the norm, and therefore we interpret it as wrong. Historically and generally, there have been and still are some frequent thematic differences that distinguish the female villain from the male villain, and she tends to wear many faces. She might be the older single woman, jealous of youth and willing to kill for it. She might be the beautiful young woman who is sexual and seductive. She is the mother. She is the stepmother. She is the godmother. She is the cackling witch who wants to steal babies and seduce men. She is too sexual, or perhaps not sexual enough. In more fantastical stories, the villain has powers we do not even understand.

But there are similarities among all these different types of female villains. She is almost always cruel and conniving and cold. She is, in one way or another, "tricking" men, either through sexuality or manipulation or marriage or any number of tools in her dastardly female toolbox. She understands and is in control of her sexuality, and she chooses to weaponize it. She usually is not good with children, in one way or another; often she doesn't even want them (the horror!).

She is, in short, not the traditional "respectable" woman, a woman who doesn't adhere to our understanding of how women should be. This is not to say the path she chose of rebellion is necessarily laudable.

Let us remember that the people writing these stories are part of the system we all grew up in; it is, as always, worth questioning what we are using as signifiers of evil and wrongness . . . and why.

There are exceptions, of course. Female comedic villains are frequently unintelligent. We are meant to laugh at their faults, many of them gendered in nature. She thinks she's sexy, but she's not. She thinks she's smart, but she couldn't be further from it. She wants the handsome male hero as her own, something we laugh at because we code her as simpering, pathetic, and out of his league.

Some women "villains," when the point of view is flipped, are simply the "other" woman, who was equally wronged by the male "hero." Sometimes a woman who is painted as villainous is in fact just being responsible ("the nagging wife," for example). (Let's be honest—that might be a whole different conversation!)

Here's an exercise. Name three iconic male villains. Now name three iconic female ones. Compare. I bet a lot, if not all, of the women you thought of are spinsters, witches, ice queens, seductresses, crazy bitches, or some other gendered descriptor.

While we are focusing on fictional villains, one of history's most infamous and notorious women serial killers, Hungarian countess Elizabeth (Erzsébet) Báthory, was accused of killing upward of 650 teenaged girls from 1585 to 1610 and, as the rumor goes, bathing in their virgin blood to keep herself young. However, despite the enduring legend, there is little to back up this rumor, and some suspect it had more to do with the fact that she was a woman who owned property—a castle at that!—and that this story was actually cooked up as politically motivated slander to get her lands.

Fairy tales (and later, animated Disney movies) really leaned into the evil witch idea. One of the lead characters in a fairy tale is often an older woman who desires beauty and youth and will kill (sometimes even eat) children to get it. The young, beautiful ingenue is often the target of her schemes. Thanks to the economic and transactional nature of marriage in early days of the institution, the stepmother frequently got wrapped up in this idea. She tended to be a manipulative woman who killed the mother of the protagonist and seduced the father in order to ultimately inherit everything he owned (remember at the time this was when inheritance and marriage—and possibly subsequent widowhood—were just about the only way a woman could own anything).

All of this teaches girls and women that, once again, their value is in their youth, looks, and desirability under the male gaze, that they have to compete with and attack other women in order to survive and thrive, that their happiness depends on their acceptance into a society where men have made all the rules. (It's worth noting, while we're focusing on a lot of Western ideology here, cultures all over the globe have similar villainesses. Baba Yaga, I'm looking at you.)

Our more recent interpretations of the woman villain include: the creepy little girl with long hair (often on the verge of becoming a sexual being); the sexy, obsessed psycho bitch; the mother (who is frequently blamed for the actions of her children); and the ice-queen bitchy boss. All these interpretations are enlightening when it comes to the question of what we view as evil and frightening in women: Burgeoning female sexuality. A woman scorned. An angry woman. Anything less than the "perfect'" mother. Ambitious women. Women who "just need to get laid" by a man to ease up.

Am I saying all the characters in these tropes are actually *not* villains? No. Many of them are, if not most. But I do think the themes emerging when we look more closely are illustrative of the larger picture of how we view the "natural" roles of women, of how we police (and fear) their bodies and any semblance of independence. More recently, many of these villainous tropes have stirred conversation. Some of our female villains are beginning to get more in-depth portrayals that flip them from villain to, if not hero, something close. Someone we can understand. Someone we might all relate to.

QUICK HISTORY LESSON ON VILLAINESSES

*Let's bring it back to bibli-*cal times with one of the originals: Eve. In Western Christianity, many of us grew up learning about Eve and how she ruined everything. When she bit into that forbidden apple, she was made responsible for getting humanity barred from paradise; the fruit itself has now become a symbol for sexuality and sin. When I was growing up and forced into endless Bible study, the implication was always that she—as a representation of all women, to be clear—was more feeble-minded and weaker than Adam; hence, she couldn't resist that temptation. She was also sexual, a quality that, for reasons I couldn't comprehend as a child, was worthy of both judgment and punishment. It was wrong, her behavior was wrong, her decision was wrong, and we all will pay, forever and always, for the original sin of Eve, the first woman ever created, at least according to the Bible.

That's a lot for a young girl to onboard. A lot of guilt and shame and, frankly, anger. A lot of internalizing of the idea that women are inherently less than, and by nature, weaker and more sinful than men.

Let's take another biblical woman, Lilith, Adam's first wife. Here's something you might not know: in some Jewish interpretations, Lilith became the mother of all monsters after refusing to submit to the missionary position. This interpretation is largely based on a medieval Jewish text called *The Alphabet of Ben Sira*, a work many historians believe was meant to be satirical. Some even believed she was a succubus—a demon that has sex with men when they're sleeping—and a baby snatcher. Fear of Lilith was such that some Jewish parents would have their children wear pendants to protect against her, since she was said to have sworn never to take a child wearing a protective amulet.

In our more modern times, Lilith has become somewhat of a feminist icon with the 1976 launch of *Lilith* magazine (tagline "'Independent, Jewish &

Frankly Feminist") and the 1997 debut of Lilith Fair, a much-beloved all-women music festival, the brainchild of Canadian singer Sarah McLachlan.

The idea of not behaving within gender and sexuality norms, not submitting to men, is a common theme with villainous women. This was part of the fear that fed into the persecution of witches, which peaked during the 1400s to 1600s. Most of the accused were women, by some accounts, over 80 percent.

The 1486 best-selling work *Malleus Maleficarum,* a witch-hunting manual written by Catholic inquisitors, contained this quote, which demonstrates the perceived sexual deviancy of witches: "When a woman thinks alone, she thinks evil.... And what then is to be thought of those witches who in this way sometimes collect male organs in great numbers, as many as twenty or thirty members together, and put them in a bird's nest, or shut them up in a box, where they move themselves like living members, and eat oats and corn, as has been seen by many and is a matter of common report?"

During this period in Europe, over one hundred thousand women accused of witchcraft died, though the number is quite possibly much higher. One of the most well known instances is, of course, the Salem witch trials of the 1600s, which led to the death of fourteen women. Many of the women accused of witchcraft lived outside society, independently, sometimes working as midwives or healers; they might have been single, or poor, or widowed, or property-owners, or perhaps all the above. Maybe they weren't religious or maybe they complained. Many were tortured, humiliatingly examined for a third nipple and a "vaginal teat" before they were killed, often by fire, beheading, or hanging.

Historians believe that a significant driver behind witch-hunting in Europe and North America had to do with controlling women's bodies and their ability to reproduce within the sanctioned family structure—anything outside accepted norm was considered a threat to the system, a system that depended on women producing children for more capital and labor, while also caring for the family without pay.

Just like poor, maligned Lilith, witches have had a feminist resurgence and reclamation. Like clockwork, with every more recent wave of feminism, there is a corresponding rise in the popularity of witches in our media.

WHY SHE MATTERS TO ME

Look, I'm frequently damn "boring" when it comes to my favorite characters. Just look at most of my fanfiction and cosplay preferences. I've been called a square for liking the "everyperson" character. But I do appreciate the power of a good villain and the often subversive, radical nature of a villainous woman. I also know there is a lot of cultural baggage to unpack with them; often their stories are about punishing other women, or they are still in service to a male character. The sexy fling for the hero. The secondary villain to the main male villain. Often, she is tricked into villainy by a man, so her evilness is not even her own choice.

What does tend to unite all those perceived villainous women is a general misunderstanding and fearfulness of women and their bodies. In the most conservative, traditional sense, "good" women are supposed to be demure, modest, humble, selfless, submissive, good with children, always putting their family first. These qualities are not inherently bad, but they do seem to be all about other people; they are qualities that, by definition, subsume the

woman's own needs, that reduce her, that make her smaller.

If we look at this history of villainous women, they don't fit into these classic boxes. As a society, we have seen a lot of growth from this; we now are finally seeing female heroes that *don't* fit this mold. We're more cognizant and skeptical of plotlines that pit women against women, almost always over a man. But still, many of these tired tropes linger.

One interesting aspect of female villains to me is how they tend to be received. In my experience, we are far more willing to not only forgive male villains but also root for them. For women, we are far, far more ready to root for their demise. Even if she's not a villain—maybe she's just annoying—we are ready and willing to cheer for an unlikeable woman's violent death, to hate her and want her punished.

One popular example often given is that of the trickster character Loki in the Marvel Cinematic Universe (MCU), who is a fan favorite villain who has appeared in multiple movies and has a show based on him. Sure, he's gotten a little ambiguous

now, in terms of his villainous ambitions, but certainly in the beginning, he leaned toward straightforward villainy and has done plenty of dark and dirty things.

Compare that to one of the first prominent MCU female villains, Hela, who did not get nearly as much fanfare and, as of now, has been in only one film, *Thor: Ragnarok.* (I adore her, by the way, and have cosplayed both her and the Winter Soldier pretty frequently. What can I say? I'm a sucker for trauma and messy black eye makeup.) However, many complained she was two-dimensional and wasn't given the room to grow, that she was lacking in the depth and consideration that the character Loki had been granted.

This is a frequent criticism when it comes to the comparison between male and female villains. Whereas male villains are repeatedly given redemption arcs and are humanized, female ones often aren't. Furthermore, the female villains are often written in such a way that the audience doesn't want to see them redeemed. In many plotlines, for example, the male villain is redeemed by the love of a woman. But the female villain is unlovable and irredeemable. Overall, more time and care are devoted to the male villains and their stories in our popular media, and this means that while we, the audience, might root for the male villain and his redemption, we tend to just want the female villain to go away.

As discussed earlier regarding the Final Girl and the Avatar, we seem far more ready to punish women for just about everything. At first, I thought it might be women who transgress outside the gender-conforming lines—who are more sexual, who are more violent, who just don't fit in the narrow box we define as women.

But the more I thought about it, the more I came to believe that our media punishes women who fit *inside* that box, too, as stereotypical and sexist as these portrayals often are. Think of the nagging wife in the sitcom. It seems the issue is more that she is a woman, and that she is not completely submitting to men or to patriarchal systems that demand she be quiet and take care of things without asking for anything.

Something else I've been ruminating over lately is the antihero, the character who is always straddling the line between hero and villain. Again, I believe we are far more willing to root for and give leeway to male antiheroes, and more ready to condemn female ones. Think back to what we discussed in the avatar section around our societal expectations of what "acceptable" revenge looks like: a white man getting violent revenge in the name of something innocent who has been wronged—whether that something is a woman, a girl, or a dog. (The fact that a house pet is in the mix is telling...)

I maintain that while I'm not condoning the violent, vengeful actions of the character Ellie in The Last of Us Part II, *I feel very strongly that a male character doing the same thing would not have attracted the same vitriol.*

On the flip side, an interesting phenomenon we've seen with the increasing popularity of true crime is the rise of women fans loving male villains—fictional, fictionalized, and not—and wanting to save them. Although that's a little outside the scope of this book, it just feels like another example of just how much room for forgiveness we give to men, and how little we give to women.

There's a reason so many fictional women villains have been reclaimed, why movies like *The Craft* and characters like Maleficent have largely female cult followings. Because in watching and admiring these female villains, we can't help but revel in the feeling of not only finding power outside conformity but potentially triumphing over it too.

THE ANTI-FEMINISM OF ACTION FIGURES

*Ever think about action fig-*ures? That billion-dollar business? It is interesting to note that we can come up with several examples of toys and merchandising influencing creative choices made in franchises. One of the most famous examples took place during the creation of *Iron Man 3*. According to director Shane Black, the studio pressured him to recast the female villain as male, which they did, while also reducing the screen time of two female characters. The reason? They figured a male villain would sell more toys.

Perhaps it doesn't even matter whether the female character is a villain or a hero. This whole idea reared its ugly head again with the hashtags #wheresnatasha, referencing a lack of *Black Widow* toys and clothing compared to toys of male superheroes from the Marvel Cinematic Universe. For *Star Wars* fans, #wheresrey started trending when Rey's character—the main character, mind you, who is a woman—didn't appear in a lot of *Star Wars: The Force Awakens* toy sets and clothes.

On the podcast *Fat Man on Batman*, television producer Paul Dini told Kevin Smith, "We need boys, but we need girls right there, one step behind the boys. Boys buy the action figures, girls buy princesses. We're not selling princesses." This is the kind of damaging messaging that is coming straight from the corporate higher-ups—they're not even pretending to toe the equality line. They are saying girls are less than, in no uncertain terms. Not worth their time, money, or concern. Secondary. "One step behind." Less valuable, full stop.

CHAPTER 5

DISABILITY RIGHTS: MAKING THE TABLE ACCESSIBLE

SMNTY WARNING

It is no longer acceptable to not have women at the table. It is no longer acceptable to not have people of color at the table. But no one thinks to see if the table is accessible.

—JUDITH HEUMANN

- Contains descriptions of ableism.

- Disclaimer: definitions and acceptable terminology around disability have evolved over the centuries.

1990. MARYLAND.

145

When the woman made it home, she contacted some friends. She needed to talk this one through. She was so disappointed and needed some support. Her three closest friends immediately offered to meet her at her favorite restaurant that night, one where the food was mediocre but reliable. But it was accessible, which was one less thing to worry about.

After they sat down and ordered a round of drinks, she launched into her story right away. How her dream job interview had managed to go downhill quickly.

"What an excuse!" one of her friends said loudly, sipping at her drink. "Total nonsense."

"If only the ADA had passed. Such garbage. Protesters literally crawled up the steps of the Capitol to show the issues with lack of accessibility, and these people, who count themselves as so liberal, so supportive of people's rights, are just like nope?!"

The woman smiled and laughed with her friend group, enjoying their full-throated support, happy to share her rage. But she was distracted. She was thinking of that lobby, of all those framed, award-winning magazine covers, of all the young people like her who had no representation, who might be isolated, who might have no access to the world they want to participate in, yes, but even just to some materials or information that might make them feel less alone.

She thought of how she used to feel: like she had to hide, like she had to "overcome" in order to blend in better, basically to make people— able-bodied people—more comfortable. She thought of all the amazing women she'd watched and studied in their writings and protests, and the fact that in the face of all the amazing, astounding work they'd done, the American public and their elected officials collectively seemed to shrug their shoulders.

She was so tired of words without actions. Of being a token.

Forcing herself to check back into the conversation, to promise herself she wouldn't give up, she smiled and laughed at her friends. They commiserated about how they'd all felt so alone growing up, in different ways, because they saw no representation of themselves in the wider world, either on the screen or in real life. The words of her interviewer echoed in her head, and she briefly marveled at how this was a legitimate excuse not to hire someone. She wondered if she could sue.

Even if she'd gotten the job, it would have taken her longer to get to work than everyone else. It would've been harder to get around. She'd have had to juggle so many things just to make everyone else more comfortable. She wouldn't have had support. Her insurance would still be higher. But she'd had hope for all the people she could reach, and all the people they could reach, and the change they could make. The awareness they all could bring.

She sipped her drink and wondered what it would have been like if the ADA had passed.

BUT THAT'S NOT WHAT HAPPENED

In 1990, the Americans with Disabilities Act *did* pass and was signed into law by George H. W. Bush. And it only came about due to the hard work of numerous inspiring, tireless, and persistent women.

The disability rights movement has long been led and suppported by women, women who were also integral to countless advances in feminism and women's rights. One of the first modern examples was Rosa May Billinghurst, who was called the "cripple suffragette" due to the fact she showed up at marches and demonstrations on an adaptive tricycle after a bout of childhood polio.

However, it wasn't until the 1970s that women began to specifically organize around disability rights. As we already know, this decade was full of social change and tumult, fresh off the heels of the civil rights movement, and the burgeoning women's liberation movement was in full swing. In the late '70s, Marilyn Hamilton invented the first lightweight, adjustable wheelchair: the "Quickie." Compared to previous models, it was highly adjustable and maneuverable. This improved the lives of numerous wheelchair users, of course, but it also changed the world of wheelchair sports for countless disabled athletes to come.

But many of these social movements were *themselves* not accessible, and the exclusionary nature of change movements and protests is an issue that remains today. Because of this, women disability rights activists frequently focused on making existing feminist resources and activities more accessible, such as recording feminist materials so that they were accessible to the blind and visually impaired. Other groups formed around the intersection of disability and lesbianism and bisexuality, addressing their lack of visibility in the feminist movement, and in general.

The increased awareness around issues like these was hugely significant in terms of broadening the reach of feminist materials and ideas, reinforcing the idea that feminism *itself* should be inclusive. As the disability movement and the women's rights movements were taking off at the same time, these women, including those from the earlier civil rights movement, were all heavily involved in each other's work.

One of the most impactful of these 1970s disability rights activists was Judith "Judy" Heumann. As a baby, Judith Heumann contracted polio. She grew up in Brooklyn, where she was banned from going to school due to her use of a wheelchair, which was determined to be a "fire hazard." The same "fire hazard" reasoning was used to prevent her from acquiring a teaching license in 1970, leading her to sue the Board of Education of the City of New York. She won the case and became the first teacher who used a wheelchair in the city. That same year, she started her own disability rights group called Disabled in Action.

Not too long after, she moved to Berkeley, California, and she, alongside Kitty Cone, Brad Lomax, and over one hundred other people with disabilities (and allies), led a twenty-five-plus-day sit-in at a federal building in San Francisco to protest the federal government's failure to consistently enforce Section 504 of the Rehabilitation Act, which put into law that federally funded programs could not discriminate against people with disabilities. As evidence of the amount of support that existed between and among different groups clamoring for change during these eventful years, the Black Panther Party provided the protesters stuck in the buildings with warm food.

This sit-in was monumental in a number of ways. It united people across a wide range of disabilities who may have previously been isolated from each other—the hearing and visually impaired, wheelchair users, those with other disabilities, and so on. It also didn't hurt that this sit-in was broadcast nationally, exposing those who might not otherwise have been aware of the wide variety of issues those with disabilities were facing.

Heumann later went on to say of this event: "It empowered us. Simply put, we were slowly moving from being a ragtag, unorganized group of disabled people . . . to a cross-disability movement. We were really recognizing that it was possible for us to envision a day when barriers of discrimination could be torn down . . . Without the voices of disabled individuals, we would not have gotten 504, the way it ultimately came out, nor would we have been able to get the ADA."

Heumann went on to cofound the World Institute on Disability in 1983, serve under both the Clinton and Obama administrations, and be the World Bank's first advisor on disability and development.

At the time, not only did some local governments have laws prohibiting hiring people with disabilities, many companies also had an unwritten understanding that they wouldn't do so. On top of hiring discrimination, issues with housing weren't much better. Accessible housing wasn't even a thing—much of the able-bodied public held a belief that it would be dangerous for people with disabilities to live alone; therefore, the options for independent living were few and far between. The mindset at the time, in the words of Mary Lou Breslin, a disability activist with polio, was: "Don't ask for accommodation. Fall down the stairs if you need to. Pretend that you're not disabled. Eschew everyone with a disability."

While the 1977 sit-in did help push the Carter administration to sign Section 504 into law, it still wasn't always enforced. All this culminated with the fight to pass the Americans with Disabilities Act (the ADA) in 1990, which was the result of numerous activists and a lot of legislative work. Patrisha Wright, who is legally blind, was so instrumental in its passage, she was nicknamed "the General." One of her first forays in disability rights was, in fact, in the sit-in, where she was acting as the personal assistant to Judith Heumann. Her experience there revealed that she had a talent in dealing and negotiating with authorities, so it inspired her to get more involved in advocacy.

As the '70s drew to a close, Wright cofounded the Disability Rights and Education and Defense Fund, or the DREDF. There, she met fellow advocates like Mary Lou Breslin and Arlene Mayerson and started working alongside them with disability rights on a national level. She became known around Washington, DC, as an expert negotiator and strategist and advocated for numerous bills around disability rights, as well as helping to organize protests to bring attention to various issues impacting the disability community.

During this time, she also met Chai R. Feldblum, who served on Wright's legal team, including as the lead attorney drafting the ADA and as the chief legal counsel between the disability community and politicians. (She also later went on to play a significant role in the ADA Amendments Act of 2008.)

One of the most dramatic protests for the passage of the ADA took place on March 12, 1990. The so-called Capitol Crawl involved one thousand protesters, including sixty who abandoned their wheelchairs, crutches, and other mobility devices to crawl up the eighty-three stone steps leading to the Capitol to demonstrate what the lack of accessibility actually looked like. The face of that protest, which was often viewed as one of the most important turning points in getting the ADA passed, was an eight-year-old girl named Jennifer Keelan. Keelan, who had cerebral palsy, told reporters at the time, "I'll take all night if I have to."

When the ADA was signed with bipartisan support on July 26, 1990, it made the US the first country in the world to guarantee by law the protection of civil rights for people with disabilities. The new law impacted an astonishing forty-three million people. The ADA made it illegal to discriminate against people with disabilities in key aspects of public life, including school, employment, and transportation. On top of that, it transformed public spaces by requiring entry ramps, automatic doors, Braille on signs, curb cuts, and lifts on city buses.

> When the ADA was signed with bipartisan support on July 26, 1990, it made the US the first country in the world to guarantee by law the protection of civil rights for people with disabilities.

The full extent of what the ADA covers may surprise you. The definition of an individual with a disability is someone who has "a physical or mental impairment that substantially limits one or more major life activities; has a record of such an impairment; or is regarded as having such an impairment." It includes even invisible disabilities—that is, very simply, disabilities that are not visible to passersby. A lot of smart people these days are writing about the problems with portraying disability only one way in our media, and how that has in turn led to prejudices on top of prejudices that *already* existed, in terms of what someone with disability looks like.

Some disability activists argue that everyone is temporarily able-bodied (TAB), making the disability community one of the largest and most diverse minorities in the world. For example, if you are a normally able-bodied person and you break your leg, you're going to be very grateful for those accessibility ramps the disability activists had to fight so hard for.

Like any law, the ADA isn't perfect. For one, it largely relies on litigation—essentially, it depends on someone filing a complaint if an entity isn't in compliance. The scenario of that disastrous job interview we started the chapter with could still happen to some extent—the difference is that it is illegal now. And that woman, had she the resources and time, could have sued and hopefully won her case.

Some disability activists argue that the ADA should not be the focal point of the fight for disability rights, that centering the act itself pushes the narrative that a person's value is determined by the work they can or cannot contribute to a capitalist system, a system that is already unequal and places the blame on the individual who doesn't succeed, despite rampant inequality. Some argue that the focus on accessibility ignores those with severe impairments and chronic illness who do not stand to benefit from physical accessibility. Others point to people with invisible disabilities as well, arguing that the main focus should be on raising cultural awareness around discrimination against those with disabilities in all aspects of life, including areas like sexual oppression and denial of rights when it comes to family. These conversations are necessary and healthy for any movement.

And the ADA has also been under attack in recent years, along with protections for those with preexisting conditions when it comes to insurance and the Affordable Care Act. During the Covid crisis, amid reports that hospitals with a limited number of ventilators had been instructed to give it to an able-bodied person over a disabled person, there have also been renewed conversations around the whole idea of eugenics when it comes to disabled people.

ARTISTS AS HEROES

 Just in case you were look- ing to learn more about the people who continue to fight for disability acts, whether through the arts or in other ways, here are a few names for you to know.

DANCER/ARTIST LISA BUFANO (1972–2013)

Bufano was an amputee, bilateral below the knee and total finger-thumb, whose love for dance and art transcended her disabilities. She danced with the AXIS Dance Company from 2006 to 2010 and was invited to perform at the John F. Kennedy Center for the Performing Arts.

She was known not only for her captivating dance and impressive athleticism but for her eye in creating art as well. One of her more well-known pieces was a dress made of unbleached muslin, with flowing tentacle-like pieces, known as the squid dress.

Bufano has been described by critics as someone who used her movement and body in dance as a specific vocabulary, in a way that challenges not only herself but her audience to see her disability, her sexuality, and her identity through her art.

ARTIST JUDITH SCOTT (1943–2005)

Scott was a phenomenal fabrics sculptor who used her art to speak for her. Scott was born in Ohio in 1943 with Down syndrome; she was also deaf, possibly due to a bout of scarlet fever. Though her family tried to keep her at home, they were eventually advised to send her to an institutionalized school in Columbus. It wasn't until 1985 that she was able to live with her twin sister outside an institutionalized setting.

When Scott enrolled in the Creative Growth Art Center in Oakland, California, in 1987, she was finally able to express herself through her artwork, using fabrics, yarn, and twine. Her art is described as "hermetic and complex, the wrapping suggests protection and concealment."

Her art is featured all over the country, including at the Museum of Modern Art, the American Folk Art Museum, and others. The Brooklyn Museum featured an exhibition of her work in 2014, *Judith Scott: Bound and Unbound.*

ARTIST LOIS CURTIS (1967–)

If you don't know her name, you may have heard about her case. Curtis, an artist from Georgia, was the plaintiff in what is now known as *Olmstead v. L. C.*, a 1999 Supreme Court case. This case helped establish the right for disabled individuals to live in "the least restrictive settings as possible."

Curtis was diagnosed with cognitive disabilities at a young age, but she was often given insufficient care and remained heavily medicated. She was institutionalized throughout much of her young life, because she was unable to get care from her home setting.

Curtis eventually contacted the Atlanta Legal Aid Society, which was able to file a lawsuit against the state of Georgia for discrimination under the ADA. After five years of appeals, the case wended its way all the way up to the Supreme Court.

Curtis, who as a result of the Supreme Court decision was finally permitted to live independently at the age of twenty-nine, has since been able to find a community of her own where she is able to have autonomy but still have a support group to help her if she needs it. She is now free to practice her art and holds exhibits in different galleries around the state of Georgia. She was even able to present a self-portrait to President Barack Obama during his presidency.

Inequality tends to look even worse through the lens of intersectionality. According to some studies of Black Americans killed by police, between one-third and one-half have a disability or are experiencing an episode of mental illness. This statistic is part of what led to the Disabled Black Lives Matter March.

As we've discussed, protesting for better treatment can sometimes itself be exclusionary and inaccessible. After the 2017 Women's March, the author and disability advocate Sonya Huber, along with others, organized the Disability March of 2017. Over three thousand people attended. This march still had its limitations in terms of who could attend, and some activists and advocates stress that much of activism is still inaccessible.

All these intersections are important, and activists loudly warn us not to ignore them. Throughout history, disability activism has touched people of all demographics, races, genders, classes, and religions. Because of that, women disability activists have been instrumental in a whole host of issues, from women's higher education access and overall legal rights to sexuality, motherhood, equal opportunity employment, and political representation.

journal entry

It's funny—even those who know me don't realize that I am someone who deals with several invisible disabilities. I also have, over the course of my life, had several temporary visible ones. In addition, I have been involved with the caring of several family members with disabilities. But for the most part, I have been relatively able-bodied and able to "get by."

But I don't want to discount the pressure I have felt to *have to* "get by." I don't want to bother anyone; I don't want anyone to know what I'm struggling with, to know the shame and anger I have around my own perceived "failings" of my body. This toxic attitude that exists throughout the history of disability activism still pervades to this day.

One thing that really resonated with me while I researched this chapter, and a topic I've been wrestling with a lot lately (ever more so during a global pandemic!), is this idea that in the US, our work ethic and ability to be productive are tied to our supposed morality. The more you can accomplish within a capitalistic system, in terms of productivity, the "better" person you are, the more value you have. That's the overriding message I've internalized, anyway. I'll work through misery, through pain, through grief, and while some of this has to do with how I manage negative emotions, a lot of it has to do with the fact that we've so closely tied "workaholism"—a problematic term itself—to something positive, something that proves you have value. This is toxic for a plethora of reasons, but it is certainly ableist, and it is clearly unhealthy overall.

I once broke an ankle while running a race, threw up, and passed out, then went on to finish the race. I even went to work for the ensuing three days before I couldn't fit my foot in my shoe anymore and was forced to go to the emergency room. This was something I was *proud* of. Look how long I could handle the pain! On top of that, I've always been hesitant to seek medical help because I have been dismissed more times than I can count.

Faking it. Not that bad. Get over it. You just want attention; you just want special treatment.

Ignoring or dismissing women's pain is a studied phenomenon, and that, along with a history of not including women in medical trials and studies, has led to a diagnosis gap for women that directly impacts quality of life. It can even be fatal. Sometimes I'm actually afraid I might die before seeking help, as are people who know me—that's how powerful this messaging is to women.

When I was fourteen, I went online and calculated how much my life cost—how much it was worth in terms of insurance. I cried and cried when I saw the number. That's part of the price of living in a capitalist society, one that values how much you can contribute to the system above all else.

While progress has been made, discrimination toward disability in the US—and around the world—is still strong, especially when it comes to women. For instance, in the US, parental leave isn't even guaranteed—we are one of the few countries that doesn't guarantee it and has no standard that employers must follow. I've had several friends tell me about how they were going to have to use short-term disability, sick days, and any number of strategies that sound completely ridiculous and horrifying when they're describing it to me, as though it's just a fact of life. Like they're just expected to figure it out on their own. Like they have to figure out how they can continue to work or either lose their job or a promotion opportunity. Like perpetuating the human species is their own damn problem.

The pandemic has shone a bright and depressing light on work- and home-life accessibility issues as well, in terms of the benefits of working from home and the institutional penalties of doing so. That's not to say working from home is easy—it isn't, especially when it comes to parents who have been expected to homeschool their children on top of managing their work. But if companies aren't going to accommodate people with disabilities, and working from home is an option, then it should be an option, and one that doesn't incur any sort of penalties.

Another issue, as with all the ideas covered in this book, is representation. I love the horror genre, but all too often the "twist" is mental illness, something that has already been stigmatized enough. In my experience, the list of examples we have of disability in entertainment consists of: (1) an angry white guy in a wheelchair looking to be cured, (2) a villain, or (3) a truly tragic figure deserving of all your pity.

These tired tropes ignore *so much* and contribute to unhealthy narratives that are already so pervasive. The kind of narratives that cause strangers to approach folks with visible disabilities with a "bless your heart attitude" to tell them "I'll pray for you." Mainly, this just makes the able-bodied person feel better about themselves and reinforces the idea that disability is something to "overcome," that someone with a disability could not possibly know joy or fulfillment. This is sometimes called "inspiration porn." For more context on this topic, check out Keah Brown's excellent book *The Pretty One: On Life, Pop Culture, Disability, and Other Reasons to Fall in Love with Me*; she explains it all far better than I ever could.

With more and more activists speaking out and continuing their advocacy, our understanding of what disability can look like is expanding. Conversations that have long been avoided are finally being had, and issues previously ignored are being discussed. It isn't always with heartening results, though I would argue at least they are happening. Still, we have a long way to go. When I think of what my workday looked like before the pandemic, a lot of it was not easily accessible, if at all. In the words of Judith Heumann, we *have* to make the table accessible if we're going to build a more equal, equitable, and feminist society.

ACTIVITY

ACROSS

2. Americans with Disability Act acronym

4. Legally blind disability rights activist _____Wright, nicknamed "the General"

6. Sonya _____, organizer of the 2017 Disability March

8. Artist referred to as L.C. in Supreme Court case *Olmstead v L.C.*

10. Major 1990 protest to push for the passage of the ADA. _____ Crawl

11. Disability rights activist with polio Mary Lou _____

12. Renowned fabrics sculptor Judith _____

13. System of raised dots, read with fingers by people with low or no vision

14. Attorney and disability rights activist _____ Mayerson

DOWN

1. Co-founder of the World Institute on Disability _____ Heumann

3. Inventor of the wheelchair Marilyn _____

5. Lead attorney drafting the ADA _____ Feldblum

7. Celebrated disabled artist and dancer Lisa _____

9. One of the earliest disability rights activists _____ Billinghurst

13. *The Pretty One* author Keah _____

interlude

‹ **WOMEN MAKING MOVES PRESENTS** ›

WHEN WOMEN RISE

T hroughout human history, women have been the backbone of so many important changes. But so often, our contributions have been minimized, ignored, forgotten, or sometimes, completely erased. Now, you know Anney and I are not ones to allow such things to happen!

Women have built powerful organizations, pulled together enormous protests, and changed the course of human history with their voices and their passion. Join us as we walk down memory lane for some of the amazing historical movements that have been led by women.

The civil rights movement got its own chapter earlier in this book; all these other moments in feminist history deserve one, too, but alas, there isn't quite enough room in these pages for everything.

This isn't a greatest hits list, nor is this a comprehensive list of all the things women have accomplished. But it is a snapshot of what women can do when they join together and let their voices be heard.

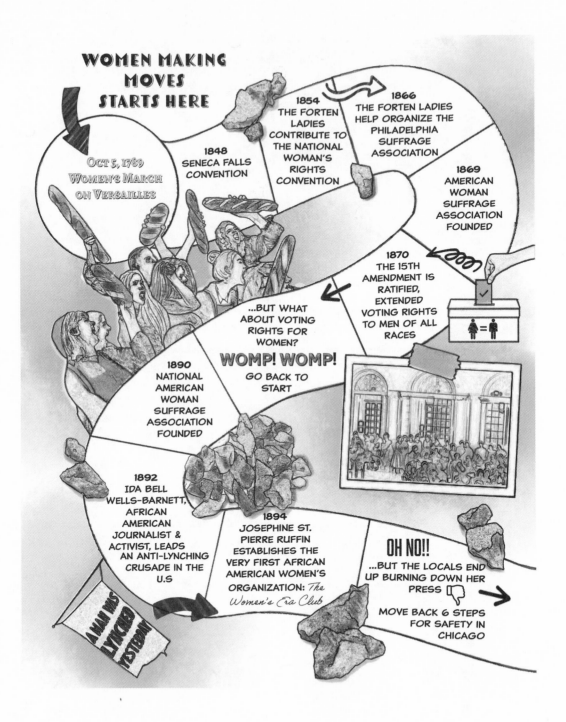

WOMEN MAKING MOVES STARTS HERE

OCT 5, 1789 WOMEN'S MARCH ON VERSAILLES

1848 SENECA FALLS CONVENTION

1854 THE FORTEN LADIES CONTRIBUTE TO THE NATIONAL WOMAN'S RIGHTS CONVENTION

1866 THE FORTEN LADIES HELP ORGANIZE THE PHILADELPHIA SUFFRAGE ASSOCIATION

1869 AMERICAN WOMAN SUFFRAGE ASSOCIATION FOUNDED

1870 THE 15TH AMENDMENT IS RATIFIED, EXTENDED VOTING RIGHTS TO MEN OF ALL RACES

...BUT WHAT ABOUT VOTING RIGHTS FOR WOMEN?

WOMP! WOMP!

GO BACK TO START

1890 NATIONAL AMERICAN WOMAN SUFFRAGE ASSOCIATION FOUNDED

1892 IDA BELL WELLS-BARNETT, AFRICAN AMERICAN JOURNALIST & ACTIVIST, LEADS AN ANTI-LYNCHING CRUSADE IN THE U.S

1894 JOSEPHINE ST. PIERRE RUFFIN ESTABLISHES THE VERY FIRST AFRICAN AMERICAN WOMEN'S ORGANIZATION: *The Women's Era Club*

OH NO!!

...BUT THE LOCALS END UP BURNING DOWN HER PRESS

MOVE BACK 6 STEPS FOR SAFETY IN CHICAGO

A MAN WAS LYNCHED YESTERDAY

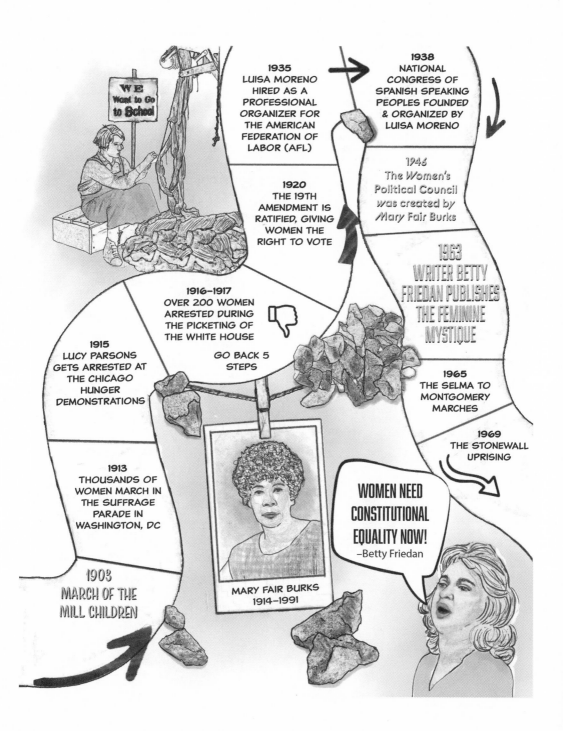

163

2006
#METOO MOVEMENT CREATED BY ACTIVIST TARANA BURKE

2008
SISTERS IN SPIRIT PUBLISH REPORT ON MISSING AND MURDERED INDIGENOUS WOMEN

2004
SISTERS IN SPIRIT WAS FOUNDED BY THE NATIVE WOMEN'S ASSOCIATION OF CANADA (NWAC)

2010
GOVERNMENT DECIDES TO DISCONTINUE FUNDING OF SISTERS IN SPIRIT INITIATIVE

1997
THE MILLION WOMAN MARCH, WASHINGTON, DC

GO BACK 4 STEPS

2020
15,000 PEOPLE MARCH IN THE BROOKLYN LIBERATION MARCH, PROTESTING ON BEHALF OF BLACK TRANS RIGHTS AND LIVES.

STOP KILLING BLACK PEOPLE
NO RACISM
ENOUGH
SILENCE IS VIOLENCE
BLACK LIVES MATTER
NO JUSTICE NO PEACE
I CAN'T BREATHE
DEFUND THE POLICE
JUSTICE FOR GEORGE FLOYD

2017
BETWEEN 3 AND 5 MILLION PEOPLE MARCH WORLDWIDE IN THE WOMEN'S MARCH, A RESPONSE TO THE ELECTION OF DONALD J. TRUMP

2015
FIRST NATIONS START GRASSROOTS EFFORT TO BRING ATTENTION TO VIOLENCE PLAGUING NATIVE COMMUNITIES

2013
Black Lives Matter created by Alicia Garza, Patrisse Cullors, and Ayọ Tometi

1979
GRACE LEE BOGGS CONTRIBUTED TO THE FOUNDING OF NATIONAL ORGANIZATION FOR AN AMERICAN REVOLUTION (NOAR)

1974
WOMEN OF ALL RED NATIONS (WARN) CREATED BY JANET MCCLOUD AND MADONNA GILBERT THUNDER HAWK

1970
50,000 WOMEN MARCH IN NEW YORK FOR THE WOMEN'S STRIKE FOR EQUALITY

1972
TITLE IX IS SIGNED INTO LAW

1973
ROE V. WADE IS PASSED

THE DOLLHOUSE

Speaking of board games! Board games have a long history of sexism when it comes to marketing, whether it's the infamous cover of the 1967 version of Battleship, which featured what we must presume to be a father and son having a grand old time playing, while the mother and daughter do dishes in the background. What about games like Mall Madness, What Shall I Be?, or Mystery Date?

A study a couple of years ago found that board games are more likely to feature a sheep on the cover than a woman.

Yep, both aliens and barnyard animals grace the cover art of board games at a higher rate than women do.

However, there have been several examples of feminist games over the years. Back in the early 1900s, there was a feminist, political board game called Suffragetto. In 1971, a game called Sexism came out. In this game, the goal was to get from the Doll House to the White House. There were cards that read: "Go back two steps because you're a woman. You might just as well get used to this."

WOMEN'S MARCH ON VERSAILLES

During the wild times of the French Revolution, when French royalty still held court at Versailles, there was a scarcity of bread—actually, an overall lack of food for the common folk. The public was getting hungry—and restless. One day in 1789, a woman began marching down the streets with a drum, which garnered the attention of others, who quickly joined in. The numbers increased until there were estimated to be thousands of people, banding together for this uncivil uprising.

Though the march began peacefully, many of the people started gathering weapons—some waved their kitchen knives, while others brandished muskets and swords. The angry mob raided the city hall to gather even more weapons, along with food and other essentials. Although the gathering had started over a lack of bread, it grew into a revolt over food scarcity, and the disgruntled masses also decided to arm themselves for the ongoing revolution. And so they did, leading eventually to the collapse of the monarchy and the beginnings of liberal democracy in France.

WOMEN'S RIGHT TO VOTE

The beginning of the women's suffrage movement can be marked by the Seneca Falls Convention. In 1848, reformist Elizabeth Cady Stanton and Lucretia Mott held a meeting to discuss women's rights. At the time, the idea of the "cult of true womanhood" dominated, which held that "true" women were pious, submissive, and dutiful to their families and husbands. But that concept was starting to fall out of favor, which is why reformists had decided to come together to discuss the need for women to be permitted to advocate for and practice their political and civil rights.

The convention itself was a two-day affair where sessions were offered for discussions, forums, and lectures for and about women and their role in society.

During this time, the Declaration of Rights and Sentiments, which was modeled after the Declaration of Independence, was created and signed by one hundred of the attendees at the convention, which included thirty-two men. Even though the convention itself was an impassioned show of female leadership, the call for suffrage was not something all the participants agreed on. It wasn't until Frederick Douglass, who was in attendance as well, made a fervent appeal that they add the right to vote to the declaration.

In 1890, the National American Woman Suffrage Association (NAWSA) was formed. It was a merging of the two most prominent existing groups fighting for the vote: the National Woman Suffrage Association (NWSA) and the American Woman Suffrage Association (AWSA). The two had been disagreeing on what they considered to be the most pertinent issues to fight for, whether it was introducing the Nineteenth Amendment or throwing their support behind the Fifteenth Amendment, which gave African American men the right to vote. There were ongoing battles about whether men should be included, and in the end, they decided to exclude Black women from their demands. (As we'll see, this deletion of Black women from widespread movements will be a trend in the years to come.)

During the fight for the vote, the women used everything at their disposal—parades, protests, and pickets—to raise their voices and bring attention to the need for equal representation. There was the Suffrage Parade of 1913, organized by the NAWSA, where thousands of women marched the parade route the day before President Woodrow Wilson did so for his inauguration.

President Wilson certainly hadn't heard the last from them. In January 1917, women's groups began picketing Wilson's White House, the first political group ever to do so. The women, who called themselves the "Silent Sentinels," continued to show up day in and day out, protesting silently, as they endured public taunts, threats, and even arrests. Over two hundred of these protesters were eventually arrested. They were placed at a workhouse in Virginia, where they were rumored to have been force-fed, which eventually led to public outrage over the treatment of the women and an even more frenzied debate over women's rights.

The Nineteenth Amendment, guaranteeing women's right to vote, was finally passed in June 1919 and ratified in August 1920. The fight had—at long last—been won.

RACISM WITHIN THE SUFFRAGE MOVEMENT

Most of the well-known leaders of the suffrage movement were, well, white women. It is disappointing to report that, despite their tireless efforts on behalf of women everywhere, the most prominent leaders were less than welcoming to the Black women who were working to fight for equal rights as well.

These women had an entirely separate set of concerns than the white leaders of the movement. Suffrage was important, sure, but they were also highly focused on the anti-lynching movement. But the white women behind the suffrage movement were unaffected by lynching laws, so they didn't seem too concerned about adding the topic to the list of rights they were fighting so hard for. If Black leaders spoke up and called out the inhumane attitudes of some of the white leaders, they would oftentimes be ostracized.

What may have been lost or overlooked at the time is that so many of the weapons used in the battle for voting rights were a direct result of the methods that made the abolitionist movement successful. Had it not been for those who used their abolitionist platforms in this new fight, the suffragette movement might never have achieved victory.

There were so many Black women whose places in history were overlooked at the time. But in recent years, some of these phenomenal women have started to receive the long-overdue respect they deserve.

THE FORTEN LADIES (1785-1914)

When it comes to legendary ladies, we couldn't bypass the women of the Forten family, one of the most prominent Black families in Philadelphia. Both mother—Charlotte Vandine Forten—and daughters—Harriet Forten Purvis and Margaretta Forten—were abolitionists and advocates for women's rights. The Forten women were founding members of the Philadelphia Female Anti-Slavery Society in 1833.

The sisters eventually helped lay the foundation of the National Woman's Rights Convention that took place in October 1854. They would also go on to help organize the Philadelphia Suffrage Association in 1866.

But the family fame was even wider than that. Their niece, Harriet (Hattie) Purvis Jr., was a leader of the Pennsylvania Woman Suffrage Association and also was a delegate for the National American Woman Suffrage Association for seven years.

And Harriet's niece was none other than Charlotte Forten Grimké, a poet, teacher, avid abolitionist, and suffragist. Grimké, who was affiliated with the

ORIGIN STORY

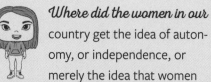

Where did the women in our country get the idea of autonomy, or independence, or merely the idea that women even deserve rights? By European standards, women had long been seen as merely the property of men. Sure, we had moved to a new land seeking independence from a tyrant across the waters, but we all knew that true independence had only been promised to the men. Women did not own land, nor were they compensated for labor; there were zero women in leadership or in politics. So how did such a radical idea form? It shouldn't be a surprise, but it might be—the roots of the feminist movement in this country started with the first peoples of the land we now call the United States.

That's right—documentation left by the ladies of the suffragette movement, like Elizabeth Cady Stanton and Matilda Joslyn Gage, showed how the customs of Native women shaped our ideas about what a perfect example of equality and equity between the sexes might look like. Many of the suffragettes were dear friends with the people of the Haudenosaunee Confederacy and would often write admiringly of the First Nations' way of life, including the example of female leadership among the communities, Native women's ability to own land and property, and the practices of a matriarchal society. These ideas were new and life-altering for the suffragettes to witness. The suffragettes' early writings, which pointed out the oppression caused by a patriarchal society, were based entirely on the Haudenosaunee's own ideas. Without the influence of the First Nations, history could have turned out differently. Alas, despite well over a century of fighting, we still have not reached the level of equality that the women of the First Nations enjoyed before we even arrived on these shores.

American Woman Suffrage Association, was an educator that volunteered to teach formerly enslaved people at Port Royal, Georgia.

Believe it or not, the line of nieces didn't stop there. Grimké would go on to teach *her* niece, Angelina Weld Grimké, who later became a distinguished writer and author. She wrote for Margaret Sanger's *Birth Control Review* (a radical feminist magazine that advocated for reproductive justice) and would be a prominent part of the Harlem Renaissance.

JOSEPHINE ST. PIERRE RUFFIN (1842-1924)

One of the Black leaders of the suffragette movement was Josephine St. Pierre Ruffin. In 1869, Ruffin, alongside Lucy Stone and Julia Ward Howe, launched the American Woman Suffrage Association, which worked exclusively on the suffrage movement, while the other organizations she was affiliated with worked on broader gender issues.

Ruffin organized the Women's Era Club, which was one of the very first African American women's organizations in 1894. She also helped found the National Association of Colored Women's Clubs (NACWC) in 1896. The NACWC's mission was dedicated to "uplifting women" as they climbed.

IDA B. WELLS-BARNETT (1862-1931)

Ida B. Wells-Barnett was active in the women's suffrage movement, as well as being an activist for the anti-lynching and abolitionist movements. Wells was a particularly fierce advocate for the Black community at the time, going so far as doing an in-depth investigation of the lynchings of Black men that continued to occur. One exposé she did on a lynching in 1892 caused such an outrage, the locals burned down her printing press, and she had to move to Chicago for her safety.

But that didn't stop her. Wells pushed to make sure that the issue of lynching and racism would be wrapped up into what was considered the main movement at that time—the suffrage movement—even if that meant she was seen as something of an outcast for refusing to back down.

Wells was one of the more prominent members of the NACWC as well, which worked to address both civil rights and women's rights issues.

MARY MCLEOD BETHUNE (1875-1955)

Mary McLeod Bethune was a teacher, a leader, a businesswoman, and a government official. After moving to Florida, where she taught as well as sold insurance, Bethune opened a boarding school named the Daytona Literary and Industrial Training Institute for Negro Girls. The school eventually became a college that, in 1929, would merge with an all-male college, Cookman Institute, to be renamed Bethune-Cookman College. Bethune would become the first Black female president of an HBCU (historically Black colleges and universities).

Bethune founded and served in many different organizations over the years. In the wake of the passing of the Nineteenth Amendment, she led voter registration drives. She became president of the NACWC and the founding president of the National Council of Negro Women in 1935.

The following year, in 1936, Bethune was appointed by President Franklin Roosevelt as the director of Negro Affairs of the National Youth Administration—and she was even known as the unofficial organizer of FDR's Black Cabinet.

Bethune fought hard to end lynching and discrimination, organizing a conference called the Problems of the Negro and Negro Youth in 1937. She was later appointed by President Harry Truman as the only woman of color at the founding conference of the United Nations in 1945.

LABOR RIGHTS MOVEMENT

The labor rights movement—which began in the 1800s and, in some ways, is still being fought today—is another giant movement that has been spearheaded by so many amazing women. And like many of the other movements we have talked about, it is a layered movement that crosses over with other injustices, such as immigration, housing, and of course, human rights in general.

Let's take a look at some of the amazing movers within the movement, whose goal was to protect the rights of workers, which included strengthening child labor laws and fighting for employee health insurance, as well as pushing for better wages, shorter hours, and safer working conditions for all.

MARY HARRIS JONES (1837-1930)

Mary Harris Jones was an Irish immigrant who was a leader and organizer for many protests and strikes in the labor movement. She became an iconic figure as she took on the role of the maternal figurehead for the movement.

After losing her entire family to yellow fever when she was thirty, Jones dressed only in black and often wore antique dresses, purposely aging herself to seem more motherly. She was known as Mother Jones, or sometimes just Mother, during the time of her activism.

Jones traveled around the country, leading strikes and protests for miners, unions, and child workers. In 1903, she organized the March of the Mill Children, a protest that stretched from Philadelphia to Long Island, which is where President Theodore Roosevelt's summer home was located.

Mother Jones's activism and leadership led to the growth of different labor unions in a variety of fields and brought attention to corrupt politicians and businesses all around the country. She was everywhere, it seemed. She was frequently hired to speak at rallies and gatherings in every corner of the country, and she also wrote articles for magazines and newspapers to rally the working people.

LUCY PARSONS (1851-1942)

Lucy Parsons was a self-proclaimed anarchist. The Chicago Police Department stated that she and her husband, Albert Parsons, were "more dangerous than a thousand rioters."

Both Parsons and her husband were activists who were deeply involved in the labor movement, as well as being activists for political prisoners, people of color, the homeless, and women. Even after her husband's death, Parsons continued to be active in writing and speaking for the labor movement and for the Socialist Party.

She also led marches for working seamstresses in Chicago and was part of the so-called Haymarket Affair, also known as the Haymarket riots or the Haymarket massacre, which took place in May 1886. Although it started as a peaceful rally in support of the eight-hour workday, the event devolved into chaos after a protester threw a bomb. Several people, police officers and protest-ers alike, were killed, and many more were wounded. Many believe that Albert Parsons, who spoke at the rally and would later be executed for conspiracy as a result, was the victim of a frame-up.

Parsons later focused her activism on poverty and unemployment and would lead more protests and hunger strikes. She was very engaged in the Chicago hun-ger demonstrations in January 1915, which led to several like-minded organiza-tions coming together for a huge protest on February 12 of that same year. Over the course of her life, Parsons was a vital part of many different activist organiza-tions, including the Industrial Workers of the World and the National Committee of the International Labor Defense. She even joined the Communist Party in 1939!

LUISA MORENO (1907-1992)

Blanca Rosa López Rodríguez, later known as Luisa Moreno, was a Guatemalan-born labor and civil rights activist. As a seamstress working in the United States, trying to help support her family, she quickly became involved with a group of Latino labor activists who worked to fight for fair labor practices. Seeing the overall harsh working conditions, the low wages and continued discrimina-tion and racial segregation, she became an advocate for equality for those in the industry. She changed her name from Rodríguez to Moreno to distance herself from her family, who disapproved of her activism.

Moreno was hired in 1935 as a professional organizer for the American Federation of Labor (AFL) but soon after joined the United Cannery, Agricultural, Packing, and Allied Workers of America (UCAPAWA), which was affiliated with the Congress of Industrial Organizations (CIO). This led to her becoming the first woman and first CIO council member of Latino heritage. Soon, she would also become the international VP for the UCAPAWA.

Moreno also became heavily involved in Hispanic civil rights. She founded and organized the National Congress of Spanish Speaking Peoples in 1938. Though she was eventually deported in 1950 because of her association with the Communist Party, she left a hefty mark on the labor and civil rights movements.

GRACE LEE BOGGS (1915-2015)

Grace Lee Boggs was a fierce advocate in fighting against the racial injustice faced by the African American community in her lifetime. As an activist within the far-left political group the Workers Party, she couldn't ignore the overlapping injustices occurring within the African American community.

She and her husband James Boggs were a powerhouse of a couple. But she didn't just speak loudly—she was known instead for being a great listener to the Black community. Sometimes she would wait in the wings for years, learning all she could from everyone else, before jumping in and playing a more active role.

Boggs and her husband would be key founders of the National Organization for an American Revolution (NOAR) in 1979. She would soon begin writing, organizing, protesting, and working with leaders like Malcolm X and other radicals of the civil rights movement.

Because of her involvement on so many controversial issues, Boggs and her husband were under FBI surveillance. At one point, there was speculation that she was "Afro-Chinese" (her parents were actually both from China) due to her extensive activity in the civil rights movement.

Although she and her husband would continue to be activists throughout their entire lives, they were not afraid to disagree with each other when it came down to tactics; nor was she afraid to break ranks with the people in their own social group.

During her time as a civil rights activist, Boggs learned to evolve, aware that the movements needed to adapt to a changing society. After the 1967 Detroit Riots, she adopted Martin Luther King Jr.'s use of nonviolent protest. She wrote in her memoir that "reality is constantly changing, and we must be wary of becoming stuck in ideas that have come out of past experiences and have lost their usefulness in the struggle to create the future."

Throughout her life, Boggs remained hyperfocused on helping her community. She would eventually develop the Detroit Summer program, which gave young volunteers in the city an opportunity to work in community gardens or become mentors.

Boggs was also very active in the labor rights movement as well. She started out as a Marxist, seeking to help those trying to find adequate housing and pushing for socialist ideals. When she was part of the Workers Party in her earlier days, she advocated for both union rights and tenants' rights. She later attributed these experiences as the impetus for her civil rights activism. Boggs spoke of how living in the unsanitary and inadequate conditions in Chicago opened her eyes to true suffering.

She became involved with the African American labor unionist A. Philip Randolph, who had organized a march to protest the segregation of military and wartime manufacturing, which ended up being cancelled when FDR issued an executive order to ban discrimination in the US defense industry. Witnessing the impact of organizations and movements like this influenced Boggs to continue in her activism. She became a key member of the Johnson-Forest Tendency, which was a Marxist-humanist organization under the Workers Party, led by C. L. R. James and Raya Dunayevskaya. She later started the newspaper *Correspondence*, which focused on the rights and efforts of the workers and labor movement.

In 1990, friends of Grace Lee and James Boggs founded the Boggs Center in Detroit, which aims to help develop new leaders and new activists and challenges them to delve into critical thinking and strategizing as organizers and changemakers.

There are plenty more movements to come. The Equal Rights Act? LGBTQ+ rights? Indigenous rights? Women have been at the helm of all these battles.

EQUAL RIGHTS FOR WOMEN

On June 30, 1966, writer Betty Friedan, the author of *The Feminine Mystique*, sat down with several women as they discussed what the next steps should be in order to ensure equal rights for all sexes. Friedan and the others had been disappointed at the dearth of results after the Third National Conference of

Commissions on the Status of Women. Taking a cue from the civil rights protests and marches, they decided to make a plan of action.

The civil rights activist and scholar Reverend Dr. Pauli Murray, whom we read about in chapter 1, was at that table. She became a key member who argued many of the different cases that would be brought in order to strike down discriminatory laws and policies within the government.

In 1970, fifty thousand women marched down Fifth Avenue in New York City in a show of support for women's equality. The protest, originally intended as a women's strike or national work stoppage, was the brainchild of Betty Friedan. This was the largest march for women since the suffrage movement fifty years earlier. And the demonstrations stretched nationwide, with women all across the country participating.

They had a specific purpose in mind—they wanted a show of strength for new-wave feminism, also known as second-wave feminism. They "agreed on a set of three specific goals, which reflected the overall spirit of second-wave feminism: free abortion on demand, equal opportunity in employment and education, and the establishment of 24/7 childcare centers."

> We women are still fighting for equal rights under the law, a century and a half after that first women's conference at Seneca Falls.

Just two years after the demonstrations, in 1972, Title IX passed, which outlawed discrimination on the basis of sex in educational programs that received federal financial assistance. And of course, *Roe v. Wade* came a year after that, in 1973.

In 1976, the National Organization of Women (NOW) organized a march for the Equal Rights Amendment, bringing sixteen thousand people to Springfield, Illinois. The following year, they held another march, in Washington, DC. But this time around, they also coordinated a run to raise money. They pulled in over $1.7 million to help support efforts toward ratification, and the next year, one hundred thousand people marched in DC for the extension to ratify the ERA. After winning that extension, the following year in Chicago they held another event called the Mother's Day March for the ERA.

As we discussed in an earlier chapter, unfortunately, the bill then ran into trouble. Toward the end of the 1970s, progress on the bill slowed, and not enough states had ratified the amendment before the 1982 deadline for full ratification. Although the ERA has been brought before every session of Congress since, it has still never been ratified in full.

We women are *still* fighting for equal rights under the law, a century and a half after that first women's conference at Seneca Falls.

STONEWALL RIOTS

In 1969, after a violent early-morning police raid on the beloved New York City gay bar the Stonewall Inn, gay, lesbian, and allied community members fought back against the police. After the six-day standoff finally ended, a new liberation movement had begun, with two transwomen of color at the helm, Marsha P. Johnson and Sylvia Rivera.

Johnson and Rivera were drag artists, both well known in their community. They used that prominence to bring much-needed attention to the needs of the LGBTQ+ community. They worked not only to spotlight the dangers faced by the LQBTQ+ community but also to create safe, nurturing environments for many who, after being abandoned by their families or cast out by conservative communities, found themselves stranded and homeless.

Despite all their activism to bring more visibility and acceptance to LGBTQ+ folks everywhere, they were fighting against discrimination themselves, day in and day out, even within their own community. In 1973, the New York City Gay Pride Parade (which began as a joyful celebration in response to the devastating Stonewall Riots) banned drag queens. But wouldn't you know . . . Johnson and Rivera were having none of that. They both marched in front of the parade with pride.

WOMEN OF ALL RED NATIONS (WARN)

After the 1968 founding then subsequent splintering of the American Indian movement, veterans of the movement and others came together to create another powerful group, the Organization of Women of All Red Nations (WARN).

WARN was created in 1974 by Janet McCloud and Madonna Gilbert Thunder Hawk, who after seeing that, for the most part, Indigenous women were being ignored, not just in the movement but in society overall, because they were seen as powerless. These women recognized that they needed a space to come together safely, especially at a time when the Indigenous community was being placed on watchlists and considered a threat by the government.

WARN began as an organization that focused on the needs of Native women and issues affecting them, but they soon expanded to include issues of prison reform and the overall culture of imprisonment for Indigenous people.

The group has also been tirelessly protesting the exploitation of the Native communities and land, in an effort to protect their own lands, resources, and the environment. They have helped to stop the uranium mining corporation that was polluting the South Dakota waters and have been a part of the protests to stop the Keystone XL pipeline.

WARN has also been a leader in advocating for the rights of Indigenous women and for improving health care, expanding reproductive rights, and seeking to end violence against women.

MISSING AND MURDERED INDIGENOUS WOMEN, GIRLS, AND TWO-SPIRIT PEOPLE (MMIWG2S)

Although MMIWG2S is not necessarily one organization, there are many people in the Indigenous community who have been fighting not only for justice but for visibility of the many women who are missing or have been murdered within the Native communities.

For so long, Native communities have been ignored when attempting to report their missing loved ones. Their tragedies have been dismissed as unimportant; if the authorities do listen, they frequently victim blame or shame the missing and their families. Many of these cases are either not acknowledged or not investigated by officials. But now, many in the community are stepping up to advocate for the numerous victims who have not been found.

More and more organizations are coming forward to seek justice for the MMIWG2S, but we want to highlight several key figures.

Sisters in Spirit was founded in 2004 by the Native Women's Association of Canada (NWAC) to get more information and data on violence against Indigenous women in Canada, statistics that were previously unknown. But they also wish to bring awareness to the growing problems of violence against Indigenous women and the many victims who continue to go missing.

Sisters in Spirit received a $5 million grant from the Status of Women Canada. They were tasked with researching and then estimating a reliable number of missing and murdered Indigenous women and girls. But they also wanted to share stories of the families of victims, spend time problem-solving the kinds of issues these communities are facing, discuss reasons for the continued violence, and find ways to keep those at risk safe.

They released their initial report, *Voices of Our Sisters in Spirit: A Report to Families and Communities*, in 2008. A second report followed in 2009. These reports offered both quantitative and qualitative data and analysis, which included stories shared by victims' families and friends, educational tool kits for communities with safety measures for Indigenous women, and outreach and support for the community.

Although the initiative was disbanded in 2010 when the government decided not to renew the funds, before they shut down, the group was able to release a new report that gave a detailed history of how colonization impacted Indigenous people. They also identified 582 women and girls who were missing or murdered during the time period of the initiative itself.

There has been some progress with the movement elsewhere in North America. In 2015, women and families of the First Nations, Indigenous people in Canada, started a grassroots effort to initiate another inquiry into the high rates of violence and murder in Native communities. And the movement spread.

The movement's hashtags, #MMIW and #MMIWG2S, began to trend, thanks to the former Grand Chief of Manitoba Keewatinowi Okimakanak Inc., Sheila North Wilson. The hashtag #MMIW made a huge impact, producing 55,400 unique uses and 156.1 million impressions on Twitter during the first national inquiry in Canada. It still generates several thousand impressions every few hours.

These social media movements have been able to bring awareness and offer a place for family and friends to share personal stories about missing loved ones. These connections have also helped give time-sensitive information for organizing, as well as encourage wellsprings of local support for the movement.

In 2018, Jodi Voice Yellowfish (a member of the Oglala Lakota, Muscogee Creek, and Cherokee Nations) and her sister, Snowy Voice, created the MMIW Texas. The group works to advocate for vulnerable Native women and safety for those who have "claimed sovereignty." The group has become a leader within organizations like the Dallas Women's March and has helped to establish resources and bring awareness and visibility to the MMIW in their community.

And it hasn't hurt the cause that, for the first time in our history, a Native person has been appointed as secretary of the interior of the United States. Secretary Debra Haaland has made it one of her missions to bring awareness and prioritize the cases of the many MMIWG2S in the country. Not only has she brought to light the need for attention to these cases, but she has gone so far as starting committees within her department to focus on the needs of the Indigenous communities, with an emphasis on MMIW and the widespread violence against Indigenous women and girls.

Sometimes it feels like things are speeding up. Do we have more to fight for, or are we just getting more and more tired of waiting? Just in the last few years, we've had some huge moments.

#METOO

The #MeToo movement was created in 2006 by the activist Tarana Burke. She started it specifically for Black women and girls and women of color in low-wealth communities who survived sexual assault or abuse, in the hope it might help them find ways of healing.

"Our vision from the beginning," as stated on the group's official website (https://metoomvmt.org), "was to address both the dearth in resources for survivors of sexual violence and to build a community of advocates, driven by survivors, who will be at the forefront of creating solutions to interrupt sexual violence in their communities."

The movement spread like wildfire, well beyond the community it was initially intended to serve. The #MeToo hashtag became a symbol of community, as well as a way of destigmatizing survivors and their experiences.

#MeToo also became a movement about accountability. Because of this movement, perpetrators like Harvey Weinstein were finally held accountable for their actions and their egregious history of abuse.

Popularity sometimes leads to problems. In this case, the mass outpouring of #MeToo stories risked the movement being accidentally hijacked and falsely credited to white women (specifically celebrities) who joined the frenzy.

But no matter, Burke has made this movement more than a mere hashtag in social media. She has indeed accomplished her goal, giving survivors a safe space to build communities, support each other, and even develop curricula to help heal so many who thought they were alone.

The movement she created has rocketed through many different industries. It has not only upended and forever changed the world of entertainment but has made an incredible impact in the food and service industries, tech industries, and beyond.

BLACK LIVES MATTER

Black Lives Matter was created in 2013 by Alicia Garza, Patrisse Cullors, and Ayọ Tometi after the acquittal of George Zimmerman for the murder of Trayvon Martin. The hashtag #blacklivesmatter was utilized as a platform to organize and bring groups together to discuss ways to push antiracism change in communities all across the country.

Beyond the hashtag, there are now forty chapters in the United States, spread out to help organize within local communities. "Black Lives Matter is an ideological and political intervention in a world where Black lives are systematically and intentionally targeted for demise," the group declares on their website. "It is an affirmation of Black folks' humanity, our contributions to this society, and our resilience in the face of deadly oppression."

The #BLM movement continues to push to weed out corrupt public officials, to fight police brutality, and to work to change policies in the federal government.

And just as #blacklivesmatter was a huge social media movement for the group's own cause, it also helped open up platforms for people to organize all around the world. The hashtag #sayhername came about not too long after, to bring attention to the many women and female-identifying people who were also dying as a result of police brutality, neglect, or vigilantism. Supporters of the movement note that victims like Sandra Bland and, more recently, Breonna Taylor, still have not gotten any justice or even as much attention as the cis male Black men who have died.

Black Trans Lives Matter is another movement that has garnered some much-needed attention for a group of people who have historically been very oppressed. The hashtag has recently been used to draw attention to the deaths of Tony McDade, Dominique Fells, and Riah Milton.

On June 14, 2020, over fifteen thousand people came together for the Brooklyn Liberation march to bring attention to the deaths of the Black trans community and rallying to show that they deserve justice. All these movements remind us over and over that, yes, Black lives matter, and Black trans lives matter, and Black women's lives matter.

THE WOMEN'S MARCH

After the 2016 presidential election, an unprecedented event took place. In response to the election of Donald Trump as president of the United States—and to the loss by Senator Hillary Clinton, who many assumed would be victorious—women all around the country came together in solidarity. They were particularly outraged after a campaign replete with blatant sexism, let alone countless credible accusations of sexual assault against the candidate.

All that anger coalesced into the Women's March, which took place on January 17, 2017. What started as a Facebook post by Teresa Shook, an angry grandmother from Hawaii, turned into an alliance of marches taking place across the country and around the world. An estimated 3 to 6 million marchers participated around the world—some put the number at 4.6 million in the US alone—making it the largest single-day march in history.

Those marching did so in protest of Trump's election, yes, but more so to support the ideals they believed in, including all those things for which we've been fighting so damn long: civil rights, LGBTQ+ rights, reproductive rights, gender equality, and women's rights in general. The peaceful

> The peaceful marches took place in large cities and small towns—an estimated 670 events in all worldwide.

marches took place in large cities and small towns—an estimated 670 events in all worldwide. The largest march took place in Washington, DC, where approximately half a million people attended. But large marches also took place in New York City, Chicago, Los Angeles, and Seattle. Pink pussy hats—an overt reference to Trump's offensive comments about pussy grabbing that surfaced during the campaign—were worn by hundreds of thousands of women everywhere.

The march did draw a lot of criticism for being very white-centered—the leaders were indeed mostly white. Even the original name, the "Million Women March," was reminiscent of the 1997 Million Woman March, which was a protest of mostly Black women against the white-dominated feminist movement. There were also critiques about mismanagement, lack of organization, and anti-Semitism in leadership, but despite all this, the march seems to have done a lot of good. In the wake of the event, many more women decided to run for office, to organize, to campaign, to form their own groups. The criticism also spurred vital discussions on the idea of intersectional feminism.

●　●　●　●　●

Is this a complete list of women coming together to make change in this world? Of course not. There are so many other movements, so many brilliant activists, and groundbreaking organizations that we would love to get into. There are so many more that are not talked about and have never been given their due. But let's call this a start.

The bottom line is, when it comes to getting things done, women do it. When we ask some of the amazing women who come on our show why they decided to do something or how they managed to pull together to confront a major societal problem, they often just respond: "I saw a need and came up with a way to solve it." That's what we do. That's what we've always done.

And to those many, many women, who have been working for decades and centuries, to try to solve all our problems, we say thank you. Thank you. We see you.

THE INVENTION OF RAPE KITS

A rape kit is meant to embody the voice of a survivor; it's meant to speak on your behalf.

—ALIZA SHVARTS

- Certified rough chapter.

- Contains discussion of sexual assault and violence.

1970. CHICAGO.

RIIING!!!
RIIING!!!
RIIING!!!

HAAA!

YOU SHOULD SMILE MORE OR YOUR FACE WILL GET STUCK THAT WAY.

WE GOT ANOTHER SEXUAL ASSAULT.

DID SHE SPIN YOU QUITE THE SAD TALE?

I JUST WISH THERE WAS SOMETHING MORE WE *COULD* DO FOR THEM. THEY COME HERE AND THEY SIT THROUGH PAINFUL, INVASIVE TREATMENT AFTER SOMETHING *TERRIBLE* AND *TRAUMATIC* HAS HAPPENED TO THEM.

AND WE JUST SEND THEM ON THEIR WAY? THEY ALWAYS ASK ME WHAT THEY SHOULD DO NEXT, THAT THE COPS DIDN'T LISTEN TO THEM, OR THAT THEY'RE AFRAID TO GO TO THEM IN THE FIRST PLACE. THAT THEY WON'T BE BELIEVED.

BUT I'M SEEING THE EVIDENCE! I HEAR IT IN THEIR VOICES! WHY WOULD ANYONE PUT THEMSELVES THROUGH THIS FOR...FOR WHAT?

ATTENTION??

The nurse never forgot the patient's question. Nor any of the following patients' questions. They rang in her head like a klaxon bell. After the doctor's distracted mention of the visitors that he had run out of the hospital, she found a short blurb in the paper about how a group of women had been approaching police precincts and medical practices across the city, trying to bring attention to the issue of sexual assault. They were telling people about something called "rape kits," trying to convince people in power why a standardized kit like this—something the hospital could turn in to law enforcement—was so badly needed.

But she soon learned, no one listened. Many of the women were jailed for trespassing and loitering. They were dismissed as loud and hysterical, stirring up trouble where they shouldn't be. Their efforts were buried.

Rather than forgetting about that patient, the nurse found herself thinking of her more and more. How could she not have had an answer for her question? How could she have done nothing to help her? It made a simmering anger burn in her bones. She was just so damn tired. Why weren't people doing anything about this? How could all these victims be ignored, their assaults simply swept away? How many weren't getting the help they needed? How many weren't seeking help at all, after getting the message loud and clear that they didn't matter? That they weren't worth helping? That absolutely no one cared?

Years and years passed—but the nurse remained just as haunted by these encounters. She and some other nurses discussed putting some protocols of their own in place based on what they'd seen and heard from patients, but their attempts to have these protocols officially recognized were continually shut down by the hospital administration. She'd even gone to the police herself, asking whether there was someone she could speak to about how to better help victims of sexual assault, in the hope of improving communications between the nurses who examined the sexual assault victim and the law enforcement officials who were handling the case. She was assured, quite condescendingly, that they knew what they were doing. That she should go home and not worry about it.

But she did worry about it. It kept her up at night, always teasing at the back of her brain.

Sometimes in the dark she couldn't help asking herself if she were assaulted, what would she do? Would anyone believe her? Would she ever get justice? Would she seek help in the first place? What about her daughter? Would even more years pass and the situation remain unchanged? She didn't have the answers to these questions. She was furious and terrified that, still, the best she could offer someone in that terrible situation was *I don't know. We can't help you.*

She wondered what had ever happened to that group of women, the ones who proposed their own solution, who had been turned away all those years earlier. She wondered what might have happened if they hadn't been shunned. If people had listened. How many hundreds—no thousands—no, hundreds of thousands of women might they have been able to help? She wondered if they were still fighting to be heard, to help give voices to others. But if so, would anyone listen?

As she examined another patient, she simply had to answer their questions the same way, with a solemn face: *No. I'm sorry. I don't know. We can't help you . . .*

BUT THAT'S NOT WHAT HAPPENED

Up until the 1970s, there had been no real advocacy for victims of sexual assault. Hospital workers meant well, but they had no real training when it came to collecting forensic evidence. They might have taken a mouth swab, wrapped patients in paper gowns, taken some information, then sent them on their way. Often, before people advocated for victim privacy, they would report their names so that they could be printed in newspapers.

However, with all the discussion around women's rights happening at the time—and yes, sexual violence can and does happen to anyone and although no one should be dismissed, it disproportionately impacts women—activists started getting louder about how poorly the system was treating victims of sexual abuse.

One woman in Chicago was particularly concerned with the issue. Her name was Martha "Marty" Goddard. She worked with gender violence issues and led Chicago's Citizens Committee for Victim Assistance. In the early 1970s, she gathered a group of feminists who were angry about police treatment of rape victims. They decided that if the police weren't going to provide what these victims needed, they'd do it themselves. But they were split on the how. Half of the room wanted nothing to do with "the man"—they didn't want to help the police, who at the time so often silenced women who were reporting assault—while the other half was of the mind that perhaps they could find a way to work together.

Goddard was determined to solve this problem, and she partnered with a professor from the University of Chicago. Together, they traveled around Illinois researching the issue and cold-calling police to ask questions about the problems and issues they faced around rape cases. The answers they collected largely centered around a lack of usable evidence. The pair then partnered up with the Chicago Crime Lab to solve this concrete problem, and Goddard began the multiyear process of creating rape kits, also called sexual assault forensic exams (SAFE).

Once she had a prototype, Goddard pulled together another group of people to help her hammer out necessary protocols and build some examples of what the kits should look like. Then they ran into a hurdle, of course: a lack of funding. At the time, almost all the grant funds they needed to access were controlled by men who really didn't think the lack of rape kits was an issue. Determined, Goddard—with the help of some friends, including one Christie Hefner, Hugh Hefner's daughter—reached out to Hefner's Playboy Foundation, which in turn agreed to fund the first ten thousand kits. The foundation also brought in retired volunteers to assemble the kits and even provided the group with folding tables and sandwiches. Just imagine an assembly line of old folks, hanging out at Playboy headquarters, putting together rape kits while eating donated sandwiches, and, yep, that's essentially what happened.

They named the kit after the police sergeant and chief microanalyst of Chicago's Crime Lab, Louis Vitullo, meaning Goddard and her collaborators hardly ever get mentioned for their contributions. Throughout the effort, Goddard and her associates had also been steadily building relationships with politicians, judges, prosecutors, police officers, investigators, and hospital employees, basically any group that might be involved in rape cases. After the kits were completed and the protocols were put in place, Goddard's group called all these allies to get them on board with the rollout of the massive training system they had in mind.

Over the next two years, this group—largely made up of women—trained over six thousand people across Illinois on proper protocols, as well as how to use the rape kits. They also took time to train hospital personnel about what trauma is and how it can present. The first kit was used in September 1978 in Illinois.

Goddard's organization shut down this training ten years later, satisfied they'd done what they set out to do. However, when rape kits started rolling out in other states, the lack of training and oversight led to myriad misunderstandings and failings, although it did at least kickstart some necessary conversations and raise awareness about the issues surrounding investigating sexual assault cases. At this point, the Department of Justice reached out to Goddard directly.

SO WHAT EXACTLY DOES
THE RAPE KIT PROCESS ENTAIL?

HERE IN THE US, it varies state to state, but in general it goes like this: after experiencing a sexual assault, the victim is advised to go to the hospital without changing clothes, which might hold vital evidence. There, the victim could conceivably wait hours before being seen. Once the victim is admitted, a nurse will conduct a medical examination, ideally in private: taking a history, making notes on the victim's appearance—visible bruises, scratches, scrapes, for example—and marking them on a diagram of a person. Then they'll use swabs to collect any hairs and fibers, as well as fingernail scrapings. They may use a colposcope, which is a high-magnification camera, to photograph the victim.

The process is incredibly invasive, not just physically but emotionally, but it is also designed to empower the victim, with constant communication about what is happening and whether they consent to the procedure. The whole process can take anywhere from one hour to over six—since these are typically nonemergency cases, how quickly they'll be seen depends on staffing and patient load. Once collected, all the evidence gets packaged up in the kit and sent off to the authorities. While the victim is supposed to be compensated for the cost of the rape kit—again, it varies state to state—they often don't, at least not in full, especially if the hospital staff isn't familiar with the process.

Even the language in these kits can vary, with some states requesting the victim's "underwear" and other states requesting their "panties." Some states even use the incredibly dated term "buggery" for forced anal penetration. Perhaps you won't be surprised to hear that these kits certainly do not allow for an accurate representation of a trans person's experience of assault.

Ideally, these kits are administered by SANE nurses, or sexual assault nurse examiners, who have been trained and accredited to conduct forensic medical exams. SANE nurses have also been properly trained in trauma and in the compensation process. However, depending on where you are, there might not be any SANE nurses around—in Georgia, for example, there are fewer than thirty in the entire state. On top of that, some hospitals will simply turn victims away, even after hours of waiting. This can happen for the very basic reason that not enough staff members are trained to—or even want to—administer a rape kit, and just an overall lack of SANE nurses across the country. Even in the most ideal circumstances—the victim isn't supposed to eat, drink, change clothes, or shower before getting the kit done—perhaps it isn't surprising that some victims will simply give up on their own after waiting hours, just wanting their terrible ordeal to be over with.

Then there's the question of what happens next. Or what's *supposed* to happen next . . .

At this point, the hospital sends the kit to the authorities for processing. The authorities test the kit. The victim also chooses whether to report the assault to the police. The authorities investigate, and if a potential perpetrator is found, they are tried in court.

However, at every step, there is the potential for breakdown and confusion about what to do next, for a variety of reasons: fear; bias; bullying; lack of education, training, oversight, and funding; issues of priority, and so on.

> At every step, there is the potential for breakdown and confusion about what to do next.

This potential for confusion is what, in part, has led to a massive nationwide backlog of rape kits. Upward of hundreds of thousands of rape kits remain untested, and some have even been destroyed before ever being tested, some mere months after being collected. There are a number of reasons—a.k.a. excuses—given for this sorry state of affairs. Lack of funding. Lack of training. Lack of personnel. Not a priority. Forty-four states don't even have a law that says when police should send kits for testing. Many have statutes of limitations on prosecution, and lengthy delays might mean missing those windows.

All these problems are exacerbated by a lack of data. What we do know, based on what is actually reported: Someone is assaulted every ninety-eight seconds in the United States. One in six American women has been the victim of rape or attempted rape. But these are almost certainly underestimates. It's hard to even get a handle on just how big the problem is, and, based on the numbers we do have, it's already frighteningly large.

> One in six American women has been the victim of rape or attempted rape.

While rape kits are a good step, they are not the be-all and end-all. They aren't foolproof. They aren't above interpretation bias. In a disheartening number of cases, in the face of solidly collected rape-kit evidence, juries still arrived at a verdict of "not guilty" because they didn't believe the woman in question could possibly have been raped. *Not pretty enough. Not the "perfect victim." They must have consented and then changed their minds.* Believe it or not, marital rape is still legal on a federal level in the US, though most states have their own law on the books. Furthermore, the entire concept of "consent" is a muddy one, flawed in legal terms and not widely enough taught to young people.

The narrative around rape kits places responsibility on the victim for preventing future rapes—it's the victim's responsibility to come forward so that the perpetrator can't rape someone else—when again, even getting a rape kit and getting it processed does not guarantee prosecution. But at the very least, for people who decide to take the traumatic step of demanding a rape kit and undergoing the difficult process, the kits should be legally required to be processed. Not doing so sends a powerful, destructive, devastating message. *You don't matter. Your assault doesn't matter.*

But processing a rape kit and ignoring the results is no better. Some numbers from the Rape, Abuse & Incest National Network (RAINN) indicate that for every 1,000 assault victims, only 4.5 cases result in a felony conviction for the perpetrator. Numbers are far worse when it comes to women of color—they face a far higher chance of not getting a conviction or their cases being dismissed altogether, if the police happen to decide there's nothing worth investigating.

The backlash against the backlog has led to some changes too—such as new laws, including the 2015 Obama-era Sexual Assault Kit Initiative (SAKI), plus a variety of new nonprofits and some new funding. In some places, this has led to increased prosecutions, including of serial rapists, which offers some new understanding of how they were able to operate and escape conviction. Findings in some counties indicate that serial rapists are far more common than previously thought. After an Ohio county tested a backlog of 5,000 rape kits in 2016, they found that, out of the 243 sexual assaults they studied, 51 percent were tied to serial offenders. Increased access to useful data like that could potentially put offenders in jail sooner, preventing them from assaulting more victims. But *only* if the kits are processed, and in a timely manner.

In other places, though, the conviction numbers have been abysmal, producing one conviction out of hundreds of rape kits. Some states have finally put into place new laws allowing victims to track their kits online, which activists hope should help keep the police departments honest about getting through their backlog.

Many of the laws put in place to protect survivors are not as ironclad as we'd like to think. Title IX, first passed in 1972, put in place guidelines around how to handle the kinds of sexual harassment faced by women at school. But it's currently under attack.

The Violence Against Women Act, also developed by activists, first passed in 1994 and amended and reauthorized in 2005 (and again in 2013), required that states provide forensic medical exams free of charge or with full medical reimbursement, even without a victim's cooperation with law enforcement investigators. But it, too, is under attack and is not always adhered to.

> Many of the laws put in place to protect survivors are not as ironclad as we'd like to think.

These delays, errors in processing and reporting, and faulty billing issues cause real-life problems. There are countless stories of survivors being charged thousands of dollars for rape kits, every bill and late-payment notice a constant reminder of what happened to them. Many victims have reported being retraumatized when they were notified over a decade later that their kit had finally been tested.

In recent years, we have seen a slew of people, largely women, speaking out about the magnitude of the problem of sexual assault. #MeToo, first started in 2006 by Black activist Tarana Burke, exploded onto the international scene in 2016 and has had ripple effects in different industries ever since. While the impact has been debated, it is safe to say that #MeToo got an important conversation started when it comes to how widespread and common sexual assault is. It also spurred public demand for more data on the topic and brought the backlog of untested rape kits into the public discourse.

Similarly, as we discussed earlier, the January 2017 Women's March, the largest single-day protest in American history, caught the public's attention in a big way. To see so many women come together to protest against a president with multiple, credible allegations of sexual harassment and assault to his name was inspiring to so many women who were victims themselves.

It is not much easier for our voices to be heard in this fight, despite all the progress. Multiple studies have found that, historically, women have not only been entirely left out of medical studies but their pain is statistically more ignored in medical settings, which leads to more negative outcomes, including death. It's no wonder that women mistrust the medical institutions that are meant to serve them.

> Multiple studies have found that, historically, women have not only been entirely left out of medical studies but their pain is statistically more ignored in medical settings.

Furthermore, high-profile sexual assault allegations like those leveled against Brock Turner or Brett Kavanaugh repeatedly remind survivors and women that they will not be believed or that they are lesser compared to the ambitions and lives of men. *How could she ruin his life like this?* Again, why are we surprised that some women give up and leave the hospital before completing their rape kit, or prefer not to submit to a traumatic police investigation, or refuse to testify against their attacker? Why, when we see, over and over again, that this type of incident so rarely ends up working in a victim's favor? That no matter how much evidence we can put forward, that we so often still are not believed?

There have been some recent positives when it comes to rape kits and rape investigation. The increased processing of backlogs has resulted in hundreds of convictions, though far fewer than one might wish, as progress on the issue varies wildly from county to county and state to state.

It is certainly true that recent news coverage has brought more awareness to the scope of this terrible issue. Another advance we can cling to is that trauma-informed training, for both medical personnel and investigators, is slowly becoming more the norm. For a long time, authorities have at best misunderstood trauma. Trauma means that victims, for example, may not remember everything clearly, that they may avoid or forget follow-ups—and our broken system only encourages these oversights. If investigators, prosecutors, and everyone else involved don't understand trauma and how it affects the brain and memory, then they cannot know the best questions to ask or how best to proceed. An increased focus on trauma-informed training throughout the system could be a big part of changing mindsets around trauma for the better.

Still, there's so much work to be done. Women have long been sounding the alarm on the damage of rape culture and the extremely high numbers of sexual assault victims, but they have been ignored or not believed, told to be quiet. Rape kits themselves were the result of victim advocates—mostly women—coming together to do something about the problem, and it was a powerful step. But still, women aren't believed, even when thousands of us share our stories on social media or come out to protest. Rape kits go unprocessed, get thrown away. When most victims of sexual assault are women, what does that say?

We're still fighting to be heard, to be believed, and to get justice. Rape kits, while important, should not be the end of the conversation. We need to face head-on the systems and structures that have allowed these distressingly high and yet still underreported numbers of sexual assaults in the first place.

REVICTIMIZING VICTIMS

When it comes to the history of protecting women, we know our past is ugly. Oftentimes survivors are revictimized repeatedly in the process of attempting to get justice. Which is particularly awful when one considers how infrequently justice is obtained.

The constant pushback victims experience when trying to get access to the evidence in a sexual assault case can make the process seem like a fight in and of itself, as you may have just read, and the burden of proof rests too heavily on the victim's shoulders.

But there are other options for recourse. The most successful way to fight for justice these days seems to be the civil lawsuit, which is a private legal action that a survivor can bring to court. It often involves seeking compensation and even punitive damage if the court finds in favor of the survivor. Unlike criminal cases, the standard of proof is not as stringent; the case does not have to be proven beyond a reasonable doubt.

Organizations like Know Your IX, which has been working with sexual assault victims on school campuses, have been working to get more information and resources for options for victims outside of the criminal court system. Sometimes, these cases result in new policies and standards even at the federal level.

The first-ever class action lawsuit for sexual harassment was brought in 1987, when three women—Lois E. Jenson, Kathleen Anderson, and Patricia S. Kosmach—filed a sexual harassment suit against Eveleth Taconite Co., a mining company in Minnesota. It all began when Jenson, as one of the first women at the company, started working at Eveleth Mines in 1975. As we all know, being a first can be an uphill battle; for Jenson, it absolutely was. She was harassed by male miners who were threatened seeing women stepping on what they perceived was their turf.

The other women had no easier of a time. Some of the men would make advances or touch them without permission. Some would even threaten and stalk the women. The women filed complaints with the company, with the unions, and even with the Minnesota Department of Human Rights. The company was told to by the state to pay $6,000 in punitive damages and $5,000 for the overall emotional damage, and they were also ordered to institute a new sexual harassment policy. Although the company complied with the policy, they refused to pay the damages, which led to the case being brought to the attorney general's office.

The case took over eight years to be resolved, and eventually the women were paid an undisclosed amount outside the court hearings. Unfortunately, one of the women died of ALS a couple of months before the case actually went to trial.

Although the women were finally compensated—something of an overall positive ending—the trial itself was a painful process, according to the records. The women had to go through painful testimony, defending themselves as they were personally attacked. The questions they were forced to answer were brutal, and they were living in constant fear of retaliation, not only from the powerful company and the men who worked there but by others who refused to see the problems of the overt sexism within the system.

They suffered, but they did manage to make such important progress. Their case has led to other large cases that have shone a spotlight on this kind of discrimination and harassment and has helped bring justice to many other survivors, making them feel less alone when facing their traumas.

We need to change a culture that instead of valuing women, dehumanizes, objectifies, and blames them, while male perpetrators shrug and say "boys will be boys." If we can do this, perhaps someday we can live in a society where a backlog of rape kits is utterly unheard of, rather than a fact of life in nearly every city and state.

As more women gain seats in Congress and other branches of government, many of them bring with them an understanding and focus on this issue. Case studies have shown that countries with more women in power report less violence. Other studies have shown that when business leaders take sexual harassment seriously, so do employees—we clearly need more women at the top across corporations and government, since women are statistically far more likely to have experienced sexual violence.

The roadblocks are everywhere, though. Sometimes sexual harassment serves to turn talented women away, a vicious and never-ending cycle. But more and more women are taking charge, running for office, leading organizations, supporting women, *winning*. The gender gap is still substantial, but the number of women in power is growing. On the issue of rape kits, among others, parity is paramount.

journal entry

In researching this chapter, I was struck by how often I read the same thing from different survivors. Sometimes it felt like I was accidentally reading the same material over and over. *Went to get the test done. No one knew what to do with it. Despite putting in the work and calling several people, no one would help me. Had to pay for the rape kit myself, even though that's illegal. My lack of payment ended up dinging my credit score. Had to explain my trauma over and over again to strangers.*

All that, and still, no conviction.

I was alarmed by how many personal friends had told me this same story too. How many of my friends broke down while we were discussing this, admitting how ashamed and helpless they felt.

I was also horrified by how many of these fears resonated with me. *Victim blaming, slut shaming. Take the evidence to shut her up, but never bother investigating. She probably asked for it anyway. No one will believe you.*

And you know what else? I was also almost embarrassed by how many things I've just taken for granted. I remember, crystal clear, like it was yesterday, walking home from the college party I'll never be able to forget. It was my freshman year, and I was numb, just thinking, *Well, my number was up.* I knew the statistics and rolled the dice. I had a drink. I was wearing a miniskirt. It was bound to happen. I brought it on myself. I was shocked, because I didn't think I was "pretty enough" for this to happen to me.

(Which, let's be honest, is an incredibly upsetting and problematic line of thought. But I did think it. Society made me think it. *That's* how insidious the patriarchy and rape culture are.)

Now the memory of that sad specter who limped home and tried to convince herself it was fine, that what had just happened to her was just a part of the college experience, makes my stomach twist and my eyes burn and my throat constrict. The child—I mean, I was barely eighteen at the time—who actually thought: *Maybe that's what dating was; maybe that's what sex was?* That was me. And in the years since then, I have paid the price for that moment, physically, mentally, emotionally, and financially. There has been a ghost hanging over me since that night.

There are smaller things, too, so insidious yet so ever present, that have been with me since that day. Every time I step outside, in the back of my head, I'm thinking: *Today could be the day someone rapes or murders me.* I always carry my license with me so that the police can identify my body if they find it. Every day. It's a part of my routine. I think twice before going out with a pony-tail because I know someone could grab it. I wear headphones to not be bothered, but they aren't playing music, because I need to be able to hear if anyone is approaching. People who love me have given me pepper spray and panic bracelets as gifts. Because they know that as a woman, just going outside can be dangerous for me. (How scary is it that this fact is so widely known and widely accepted, that people can make a Christmas gift out of our terror?)

Still, we don't believe women. We seem to accept, at the societal level, that sexual assault happens, enough so that we will offer gifts like pepper spray to women with a smile and a ribbon. I can't imagine my brothers have ever received such a gift. With this sort of casual societal acceptance of the threat of violence, we are putting the responsibility on women—*here's your pepper spray; it's on you to keep yourself safe*—rather than trying to deal with rape culture head-on.

And whenever it comes down to deciding whether a woman's trauma, healing, and future or a man's future and freedom are more important, juries and authorities have chosen the man's future again and again and again. *Come on. He's a good guy. You don't want to ruin his life, do you?* Never mind the impact on women's lives. Never mind the message that sends, a message reinforced in all kinds of ways—by the media, in the enforcement of dress codes, in the news we see every single day.

This is your fault. You are the gatekeeper. Men can't help themselves. Sex is *owed. Entitled.*

I think about the various times I've had to de-escalate situations when men have approached me sexually, and it disturbs me. Often I will laugh gently, as if we are all having a good time but won't turn them down directly because I'm afraid for my safety. Then I know I will be told that it was my fault, because I didn't tell him no. Then I think about the various times I've been screamed at in my face, followed home, grabbed, threatened, for *saying* no, and for trying to let them down easy because they couldn't hear no.

I think of all the rules I've implemented to keep myself safe and to never ever send the wrong signals, or even just signals that could possibly be misinterpreted, and how these rules limit me and my sexual wants and desires. I think about the fact that no matter what I do, or say, or wear, or decide, I will always be blamed.

I think about how hard it is to convince yourself it isn't your fault in the face of *all of this*. Because of this narrative, one that is driven into us so often, from so many angles, I realize that for as long as I can remember, I've been afraid of my own body and the attention it gets, or doesn't get. Why? Because women's sexual desire is our worth, but it is also the thing that you are blamed for in sexual assault situations.

Women's bodies have a long history of being policed and judged and blamed. You have to look a certain way—thin, white, young. Ageism, racism, and fat phobia are, of course, entrenched in our society; the world is constantly telling us that we are not good enough, that our bodies do not meet this standard society tells us is "perfect," and that you brought any assault on yourself.

Which goes back to the thought that kept going through my head the night I was assaulted freshman year: that there was no way anyone would assault me because I'm not pretty enough. The fact that I remember thinking this frightens me so much. It was because of this sick belief that I developed an eating disorder. As a result of this twisted mindset, I structured my life and did so much damage to my body and mind because I thought I needed to look a certain way. Which is even wilder when you think about the fact that I didn't even want the attention that looking a certain way would grant me.

But I saw again and again that traditional beauty and youth were women's currency. It's how we compliment young girls. *You look so pretty.* Is it any wonder I now have anxiety about any compliments I receive about my looks?

Compliments, no matter how polite and well meaning, make me want to scrub my skin and hide away. No matter how my body looks, I struggle with the feeling it's not *mine*. That it draws attention, that it is dangerous, and that makes me hate it. That makes me hate *me*.

It's exhausting, chasing a body I've been told I should have, but that I don't have and may be impossible for me anyway, and then blaming myself for it all. Looking at myself in the mirror and telling myself I matter, that it wasn't my fault, when so much of our discourse is telling me the opposite. It wears me down. It wears so many of us down. In my most tired moments, it makes me feel like I'm in the wrong, I'm the monster; maybe I should just give in. Maybe that it would all hurt less. Maybe it didn't matter. Maybe *I* didn't matter.

Working on this chapter made me think a lot about consent, too, and how, if we live in a society where "no" isn't always, *always*, safe, or respected, or okay—whether we are in a relationship or not—if marital rape is a thing that exists at all and there are some places where it is perfectly legal, then we've got a lot of damn work to do.

But I've also been struck by women like Marty Goddard and Tarana Burke, women who have seen a profound problem that is impacting their communities and decided to do something about it when no one else was. Doing the research, doing that work, making their voices heard. I'm struck by the countless brave people who have shared their stories with the hashtag #MeToo, calling for accountability, calling for action, calling for change.

That quote at the beginning of this chapter? In 2020, after decades of research, Aliza Shvarts debuted a piece of artwork called *Anthem*, which featured dozens of rape kits from various states. They came in a wide range of sizes, with different items and instructions, revealing in stark detail the lack of consensus on the federal level about what to do about sexual assault.

Sometimes I am utterly heartbroken and defeated by how many of us there are. Other times, I am heartened and uplifted at the community we've formed to change things and the support we've provided each other.

THIS CHAPTER DOESN'T DESERVE
AN UPLIFTING ACTIVITY.
THIS ONE REQUIRES WORK.

Here are some resources to use and organizations to support if you'd like to make your voice heard:

- Rape Abuse & Incest National Network (RAINN)—www.rainn.org

- National Sexual Assault Hotline: 800-656-HOPE

- National Sexual Violence Resource Center (NSVRC)—www.nsvrc.org

- Victim Connect Resource Center—www.victimconnect.org

- End the Backlog— www.endthebacklog.org. This program of the nonprofit Joyful Heart Foundation, founded by Mariska Hargitay of NBC's *Law and Order: Special Victims Unit*, is dedicated to ending the rape kit backlog.

ACTIVITY

The Mary Sue

NAME: Mary Sue

BIO: Idealized version of the writer and beloved by all. Beautiful (not too beautiful!), though they don't know it. Young, thin, delicate, high cheekbones. Soulful, captivating eyes. Long hair that falls into their face. Shy, clumsy, "fiery," sweet, good, funny, endearing, good at pretty much everything except walking and taking care of themselves. Style could be goth or quirky, though a magical movie makeover may be on the horizon. Center of the story, target of every villain and love of every hero (and some villains too). Almost dies on a regular basis. Believes they are undeserving of love and the guy of their dreams, but with time and perseverance, he convinces them otherwise. At some point they sing at a concert, surprising everyone with their stunning voice. Saves the world over and over using the incredible arsenal of powers and training they have, at great pain to themself.

FICTIONAL WOMEN PRESENTS

LET US TALK ABOUT THE MUCH-MALIGNED MARY SUE.

FAN FICTION is a category I feel extremely well versed in. I'm fairly certain I could teach a class on it, including all the tropes therein, and most importantly perhaps, on why fan fiction matters. Very quick definition: fan fiction is essentially what it sounds like—fiction written by fans of a preexisting property, about an alternate storyline related to said preexisting property, that is then posted online or elsewhere, read, and reviewed by other fans. It is often discursive and is a way for fans to engage with a fandom, and for the fans themselves to create content in the face of mainstream media that often erases them. Because of the community aspect, writers generally have to be aware of how what they are writing might impact the reader; readers can and do leave direct comments to the writer if they feel the writer isn't doing just that.

Although I would argue that about 78 percent of most popular entertainment created within franchises is essentially fan fiction (which includes a bunch of critically lauded books and shows and films that might surprise you as well), it is still viewed as frivolous and silly at best, and as disturbing and worthy of derision at worst. Unless a man does it—well then, that's academic and will be published and accepted! A woman? Get outta here; that's fan fiction and therefore worthless!

I could talk about fan fiction forever, because the whole process fascinates me on a number of levels, but I digress. Back to Mary Sue! A Mary Sue is essentially a fantasy placeholder character, someone, usually a woman, who is too perfect, lacks flaws, lacks depth, is maybe kind of boring, and is typically viewed as an idealized version of the author. If I had to expound on it, she's usually beautiful, sweet, charming, shy, clumsy, powerful, brave, and loved by everyone (except maybe her abusive family—note: traumatic backstory alert). A Mary Sue, in fan fiction, is usually an original character, or an OC, of the author's creation introduced into a preexisting fandom.

The term "Mary Sue" was first coined in a Star Trek *fan zine in 1973 by Paula Smith. Closely related terms are the "Manic Pixie Dream Girl" and the "Cool Girl."*

If you would like to learn more about my absolute favorite trope, the cinnamon roll (too sweet, too pure, too innocent for this world, basically a gosh-darn sweetheart) and what it has to do with trauma, go check out the podcast episodes we did on it—"Cinnamon Roll," "Happy Hour #4: Cinnamon Roll," and "Happy Hour #28: You Can Be Happy, Cinnamon Roll!"

If you're thinking those words sound like they could describe a male hero, you get a gold star. More on that in a second!

There are legitimate criticisms to be made about lack of character development and lazy writing in commercial entertainment, but when looking at fan fiction specifically, plenty of criticisms miss the point, are done in bad faith, and are particularly revealing of our thoughts around the tastes of girls in particular.

First of all, fan fiction is a *hobby*. Sure, some people have managed to turn it into a career through one avenue or another. But at its core, fan fiction is a hobby that people aren't being paid for. The community aspect of this hobby is a key part of people's engagement with it. Fanfic authors sometimes are looking for constructive criticism or ways to improve their writing, but sometimes they're not. In my opinion, young girls or even women writing Mary Sues makes sense. It's *nice* to write a story where everyone loves you, where you're good at everything even if you're a bit of a klutz, where you're beautiful and desired.

To me, writing this kind of positivity in the face of all the harmful messaging we get about how our bodies should look and how we should be—things that are impossible to achieve for most of us—is exactly what we should be doing. It's one way of coping with all those toxic ideas and trying to convince yourself you are worthy and loveable, even if you are constantly fighting so hard to believe it yourself. It's a way to remind yourself that you, too, could do amazing things.

Many of the authors of Mary Sues are young girls who are going through adolescence and working through their thoughts on big things like sexuality and consent, ideas that we in the US largely don't teach, and sometimes even slut shame and mock girls for asking about and exploring. We, as a society, are *terrified* of young girls' sexuality. Fan fiction is a space where authors, who are mostly women and are therefore well aware that women experience significantly higher rates of sexual assault than men, are very careful about labeling content. They use tools like tagging and author's notes in order to keep the community—which is held in the highest regard—and their readers safe. This type of forum, it turns out, has been great for conversations about what is consent and what is not. (We did a podcast on this idea—"DubCon," or dubious consent. You should give it a listen.)

Second, part of the fun of writing fan fiction is that it doesn't necessarily have to be, from a critical standpoint, "good"—and frankly, it's worth questioning who gets to decide what "good" is anyway. Fan fiction can be something that doesn't make sense, or has been written somewhat hastily, or gets to the part everyone wants to get to without all the other boring plot-point/backstory stuff. In the fan fiction realm, you're entering a sandbox that you and the readers already know, so you get to play around there without having to do too much worldbuilding. Don't get me wrong, I have read some *amazing* fan fiction that I truly believe is better than the original work. But it doesn't *have* to be that. There's no studio breathing down your neck, pressuring you to do something that pleases *everyone*. It can be something niche, and I'm talking *so* niche*, just something for you and other fans like you to enjoy.

Third, we humans have a *long*, sordid history of making fun of teenage girls and the things they like, especially if it has to do with sexuality. The Beatles weren't cool when it was young women showing up for them—no, it wasn't until men, and male critics, started digging them that they were deemed legitimate musicians worthy of praise. The language we use to talk about fangirls (and the related "fake geek girl" who supposedly only likes what she likes to trick men into dating her) can be outright dismissive and derisive, even fearmongering. We feel perfectly comfortable mocking and deriding the Mary Sue because the trope is associated with teenage girls, and we have long accepted that it is all right to make fun of them and their tastes. All this is tied into—say it with me now—sexism!

 Funnily enough, I'm very sensitive to writing that doesn't "earn" the emotions they're telling me I should be having, that isn't genuine. It turns me off so quickly. This is slightly different from a Mary Sue, at least in terms of its mainstream usage. It's less that they're telling you how to feel emotionally and more that they're just not necessarily giving the character as much depth. It results in a character that many view as flat and perhaps goody-two-shoes.

Basically it's an unearned emotional manipulation. This might sound confusing, but I promise, I can sense it!

Now the term Mary Sue has gone mainstream. Critics, both professional and not, use it to denote something unbelievable. Rey from *Star Wars*? Mary Sue, no way she'd be that good that fast! (Why don't we ever ask if Kylo Ren just sucked??) Arya Stark killing the Night King in television series *Game of Thrones*? Hell no, that's a Mary Sue. (Ummm, did we watch the same show? She trained for, like, *the entire series*.) Again, having opinions and criticizing characterization is one thing, but using the gendered term Mary Sue to dismiss a female character is pretty telling. What it implies is that the reader or viewer cannot *believe* a woman *could possibly* be the hero, the one to save the day, the center of a storyline that doesn't principally involve her body and its attractiveness to men. The "hero" space has for so long been occupied by male characters that it's almost as if the reader/consumer can't even process this information, and in holding such ideas at bay, these viewers, uninterested in progress, are doing their damnedest to gatekeep, to preserve things the way they always have been, the way they think they always should be.

Oh, and there's a reason for all this. For an unfortunate amount of time, most female characters in the mainstream were written by men; as a result, their stories often just weren't given the attention, depth, or complexity that a man's story would.

At this point, you may be asking yourself: Is there a male equivalent term to the Mary Sue? There is: the Gary Stu, or Marty Stu. But none of them went mainstream. Isn't that interesting? Occasionally, the term Mary Sue is applied to male characters, but overwhelmingly, it is used for women. And yet, there are *plenty* of male characters who qualify as a Mary Sue—I thought of at least ten popular ones while writing this paragraph. (I mean, spend some time thinking about Clark Kent, if you will . . .)

The difference is they're men, and they are allowed to be perfect. For women, this is a quality we are not permitted to attain, or even attempt. Men can be perfect and brave and heroic. Women can, too, but then they'll be dismissed as a Mary Sue. *Not believable.* What is applauded in a man is demonized and dismissed as unbelievable in a woman. With every intersection therein, the more quickly the label gets slapped on. Be quiet and go back to being a supporting character, we are told, a sexual object for men to enjoy.

I wonder if the Mary Sue is held to higher standards—she must be more perfect—because we hold women at large to higher standards?

BIGGER PICTURE

Since its inception, fan fiction has been a space that has been run by marginalized communities, and particularly women. From papers in the 1800s, fanzines in the 1900s, and with the advent of the internet in our homes in the 1990s, online fan fiction communities, women have been running, writing, and reading fan fiction. They saw a space that was missing—representation in both entertainment and technology—and created it. When the nonprofit AO3, one of the largest fan fiction sites, was coded, it was the largest majority-female independent coding project ever.

Women and marginalized people have long been the innovators of so much of the technology and internet we use today, though their stories are so rarely told. You've got Ada Lovelace writing the first algorithm for an early mechanical computer. You've got Grace Hopper inventing the first code compiler and, with the help of a team, writing the first programming language to use words instead of numbers (COBOL, a programming language still used today!).

Speaking of the internet! We wouldn't even have such a thing without Radia Perlman, the "Mother of the Internet," and her spanning tree protocol (STP), which created a direct path between active networks, basically allowing for connection. The very first social media network? It was created by Stacy Horn in 1990.

And so many times, we have seen Black women be the force behind popular technology platforms, both technically and creatively, only for these platforms to get appropriated, their contributions erased.

At one time, women made up a majority of people in the computer field. What changed? Money. When it became a lucrative field to be in, women were forced out.

Men have made themselves the center of this story—all the stories, in fact. They can be the hero. But as we've seen, if a woman tries? She's dismissed as a Mary Sue. There are exceptions of course, but this is how we've seen the narrative play out all too often. There has already been some work to reclaim this term (including the website TheMarySue.com). But I think it's time we change what it means.

Maybe a Mary Sue is just someone who is good at what she does, whether in the fictional or real world, and it's about time we recognize it. Or perhaps when we tell a story, we are asking the audience to suspend their disbelief and have a little fun with the female as well as the male characters. After all, that's something we've long done for men—suspend our disbelief and just lose ourselves in the story. Maybe it's time we do the same for women.

WOC SIDEKICKS AND SBFS

 I love movies, books, and all the different entertainment outlets that let me escape my current reality. So much so that I am obsessed with my comfort series, you know, the ones that you watch on repeat and oftentimes are the projections of the emotions you're feeling or the emotions you're trying to ignore.

Growing up, I lived in the world of musicals, rom-coms, series like *Anne of Green Gables*, and so many of the Disney movies that I think fondly of. But as a Korean adoptee in the white world of North Georgia, I rarely saw any type of representation of someone like me. I mean, I was one of two Asian girls in our school, and my need to fit in would often push me to stay away from anything that seemed remotely Asian. It took so long for me to figure out why. In a world that was spouting off about the necessity of being a melting pot and

assimilating, I wanted to follow suit. All I wanted was to fit in. And for me that meant being invisible, being the model minority, if you will.

And that's what I knew. All the representations I saw, whether in a TV series, a movie, a music video, all of them told me this was my role, to be in the background or, at best, a sidekick/comedic relief for the main cis, white, hetero protagonist. And I fed into that in my real life too. The Woman of Color Sidekick. I was always the WOC Sidekick to my white friends, the comic relief, the one who made jokes at my own expense to appease and ease those whose privilege always put them in the starring role.

And though things are slowly shifting, with movies like *Shang-Chi, To All the Boys I've Loved Before*, and *Eternals*, it's still very obvious that change is slow and, man, sometimes it drags. Watching the movie *Joy Luck Club* many years ago allowed me a moment of seeing someone similar to me, even though they were not the same ethnicity. It still felt so disconnected, because it wasn't my experience. But in some sense, I did finally feel seen.

Of course, more often than not, I was used to shows like the *Gilmore Girls*, with characters like Lane Kim, the fast-talking best friend who is often the helper of the main girl, Rory. And this is still happening! You see it in shows like *Emily in Paris* (which has been criticized for a *lot* of other reasons); it's the same old trope: Mindy Chen has a better storyline than others, but she's nonetheless the WOC Sidekick.

And then there is the overused Sassy Black Friend (SBF). Remember beloved movies like *Clueless*, with characters like Dionne, who was the best friend of main character Cher? Or the many different characters in some of our favorite sitcoms, like Donna from *Parks and Rec*, who has often

been compared to the highly offensive "Mammy" character from days past. The trope is tired and racist and, once again, used to relegate Black women to background characters.

Of course, the racism behind the erasure or stereotypical usage of marginalized people has an effect on so many. When we look at the oversexualization of Black, Latina, and Asian women, it is rampant. According to one study done in 2019 by the Geena Davis Institute on Gender in Media, Black women and other women of color are more likely to be shown as partially or fully nude than white women by at least 5 percent, which is shocking since white women are typically given more roles and more screen time than women of color.

There has been a bit of an increase in women on screen but, no surprise, that's due to the slight increase of white women on screen. In 2020, white women made up at least 68 percent of the women on screen, while 20 percent are Black women and, down a bit further, are Asian women at 7 percent.

Is it changing? God knows, I would love to see it change. With movies like *Encanto*, *Turning Red*, and *Black Panther* and shows like *Insecure* and *Fresh Off the Boat*, we are seeing progress. At the very least, we are starting to see deeper characters being offered to WOC, still marginalized, but improving.

But we are far from getting to a point of good representation, whether that is the characters that are being written or the people who are representing them. (Not even going to start with the whole white-washing of characters—hello, ScarJo and *Ghost in the Shell*).

If you look at the most popular and critically acclaimed movies from the past several decades, there are hardly any movies headlined by women of color: one top films list I found online had a movie starring Penelope Cruz and one movie with Gabourey Sidibe. That's it.

It is exhausting to examine how often our society ignores marginalized people altogether. If they are represented at all, they are seen as a perfect caricature of whatever funny stereotype they might embody that will put the watcher at ease.

Part of the solution is having diverse voices telling their stories, celebrating every culture, and allowing more individuals to be the main character who we get to see grow, learn, and love. We need more WOC to be an accurate representation of what it means to be a woman today, in all our colors and shapes and sizes.

Let's hope that one day, the many marginalized voices who have been begging for a seat at the writers' table will finally get their shot. Let's hope that we will soon see all the many talented actors show up on our screens, the ones who have been waiting so long to have the same opportunities as their white counterparts to tell their own stories.

WHY SHE MATTERS TO ME

While it may seem like I am mocking the Mary Sue at the top, I am not. If anything, this is a love letter. I wrote a Mary Sue when I was in high school. She was a messy goth everyone loved and took a bullet for Billie Joe Armstrong of the band Green Day, on whom I had a huge crush at the time. Turns out, she was amazing at singing and guitar too!

Was it good writing? No, though I like to think it had some redeeming qualities. Did it help me work through some stuff I was dealing with in adolescence? Yes. Did I burn it so no one could ever read it? Yes. Do I regret that? Also yes.

As I've told you, I even dressed as a Mary Sue I created when I was eight. Her name was Terra Polaris, and she was the best Jedi to ever have existed, thank you very much.

I've read fan fiction since middle school. Fan fiction, if I'm honest, is what got me through the pandemic. It helped me learn to be a better writer, and it made me more aware of how my writing would be perceived. Fan fiction helped me learn more about myself and helped me work through some of my trauma. It is a love of my life.

For me, fan fiction is a space to safely (for the most part) explore ideas and thoughts, to create representations of yourself in your favorite media where they don't exist. I've seen the medium change and grow and become more inclusive and aware, though of course, there is still plenty of room for improvement. I've seen the argument around the Mary Sue change and diminish—the phrase used to be a death knell for a character, the worst critique one could receive. Now? Not so much.

I think stories can have a "Mary Sue" and still be enjoyable and worthwhile. God knows we've been enjoying male Mary Sues for a while without comment.

Look, I'm not saying there aren't some absolutely cringe-worthy Mary Sues out there, though I might argue unless you've read fan fiction, and a lot of it, you don't even know how bad a Mary Sue can get. In fact, when people tell me they think Rey is a Mary Sue, I blink at them, staring blankly. Oh, they just mean a woman who is a hero character. So dismissive. So wrong.

A Mary Sue is so different in my mind. It's not a bad thing to recognize tropes and critique them and push past them (though not all are necessarily bad). It's true that often, a Mary Sue could use more complexity and depth. But there is so much latent sexism wrapped up in the term Mary Sue, and the derision inherent in the term shines a light on our societal fear of burgeoning sexuality in young women. We have spent far too long cruelly dismissing the likes of teen girls. (Mistake. BIG mistake. I mean, who wants to mess with a pack of Swifties??) We have been far too willing to give so much allowance to men and male characters, while affording women and woman characters absolutely nothing. Heaven forbid you have any other marginalized intersection. It's time we recognize women can be heroes, without dismissing their accomplishments as unlikely, absurd. Because I believe a Mary Sue can certainly save the damn day.

I mean, that girl (me) who wrote a really cringeworthy Mary Sue? Guess what. She grew up and wrote a BOOK.

216

CONCLUSION

SAMANTHA: Anney, when it comes to what we do, you know, podcasting and researching and writing and talking to all kinds of different interesting people, you and I have had a lot of conversations about why we do it. We talk a lot about our insecurities, our hopes, and our goals.

When we were first told that we would be writing a book based on our podcast *Stuff Mom Never Told You*, we sat down together to talk about what we wanted to accomplish with the book (after the panic attack had subsided, that is). One of the things we said, I think, to reassure each other, was that we need books like this. I think sometimes we, like a lot of women, get frustrated by how slow progress feels. But books like this remind us how hard this work is, how much effort is required, and by *so* many, to make progress happen. We also hoped that the whole book-writing process would help us grow in our own feminist journeys, right? And that maybe, just maybe, it might help our readers do the same.

ANNEY: Yeah, I think you're right, Samantha. I grew up reading books, getting lost in other universes, and being exposed to new ideas and ways of thinking—or at least, they were new to me. I also grew up in a small town, so all my escapist reading was one of the only things I could find that made me feel a little less alone. That someone else out there, at some point, thought the way I did, *felt* the way I did.

But I also had a long way to go in terms of unlearning so much of the toxic soup I'd internalized, to work on becoming more of an intersectional feminist. When I first started working on the *Stuff Mom Never Told You* podcast, I remember so clearly thinking, *I wish I had had this growing up.* I wish I'd had voices in my ear talking about so much of this stuff, especially when I was sitting alone in my room, wrestling with so many overwhelming questions and feelings. It felt like the world kept telling me I was wrong for how I felt, for questioning, for *existing*.

Through the work you and I have done together, I have heard from so many people, from all backgrounds, who felt similarly, who felt so much relief at finding something that assured them they weren't alone.

While there are similarities, writing a book is for the most part radically different from recording a podcast. In some ways, it's scarier to have to write something out and see the physical evidence of your words. On top of that, writing is a very different medium than podcasting. I'm a firm believer that though there certainly is some overlap, not everyone who is into podcasts is into books, and vice versa. We want as many people as possible to learn about intersectional feminism, and we do not want to leave anyone out. Writing a book was part of that goal.

When I think back to all the amazing, powerful, revolutionary feminist books that have impacted my life and changed my worldview, books and writers that have informed my work and given me tools to recognize all the things I need to unlearn, and all the things I need to build upon, I'm forever grateful. It's a bone-deep, in-your-soul kind of gratitude. I can only hope that this book can do at least a tiny little bit of that, that it might reach some young people who are alone in their rooms, that it might expand some horizons for others to build upon for the next generation.

SAMANTHA: I agree 100 percent. Trying to unlearn the misogynistic leanings that are the underpinnings of our society, it's a lot of work. I hope having books like these, so we better understand our history—not just the good parts but the bad and ugly parts too—will help us learn the truth about our past. We need to get to know the many incredible women in history who have so often been left out, so we can give credit to those who have fought so hard for us. It's an ongoing battle.

To be honest, writing this book was taxing. The insecurities that you talk about, of just existing, are such an ingrained part of being a woman in our society. Women have been told since the beginning of time that existing as a woman is a privilege given by man, and that in order to be a good partner/human, we must remain as small as possible, to stay in the background. The reason it is so important that we shine a light on the works of these incredible women and talk about the continued injustices that need to be addressed and acknowledged is so that we, as a community, can help correct the system. This system, that has oppressed so many for so long—we need to keep believing we can fix it. We have to keep talking about its problems, its weak spots, its failures; we need keep to pushing it forward, and we can never stop.

This book journey has been a bit of a winding road. For me, it felt overwhelming. My background is in social work, a job that is all about being in the field and working with the messiness of human lives. I frankly felt underqualified talking about these amazing folks and the different policies and movements that people have been working so hard on, some of whom have been doing so since way before we were born. Trying to make sure we have everything correct and making sure that we are giving those people who have spent their lives fighting for equality and freedom their due for all their work? It feels like such a huge responsibility. And trying to do it in a way that is respectful to all was something that was incredibly important to us. We hope we have done that. What was the most difficult part for you, Anney?

ANNEY: The most challenging bit for me was not writing the entire book on Princess Leia. Joking! Sort of. That really was a challenge. But truly, it was overcoming my fear of not doing justice to the inspiring women who have been so instrumental to the feminist movement—and have oftentimes, as we keep pointing out, not been given the respect and recognition they deserve. (Also, getting something wrong. I'm still scared about that. We tried very hard not to, but history is messy and complicated, so there is always a risk.)

Every decision we made about what should appear in this book felt like a disservice to something or someone else. There is so much work that has gone into intersectional feminism, and so many people behind that work, that many of them, by necessity, have been left out of the narrative. We wanted to do what we could to fix that, but it was a daunting task.

The fact that so many of the subjects we did choose to cover are currently under attack and at risk, at this very moment, that was also difficult. A lot of days it was hard not to wonder if the hard work of all of these people is just eroding away. Some days, I felt like just hunching in on myself, thinking, *All this progress, God, it's just being erased.*

Also. Deadlines. Ugh. They were hard too.

SAMANTHA: And since we've talked about the challenges, what did you find rewarding in this experience?

ANNEY: As stressful as the experience of writing a book has been, there were plenty of rewarding things too. I will forever be thankful for my friends and family who supported me, who listened to my anxieties and fears, as well as my excitement and a *lot* of random facts. That support was invaluable and inspiring.

On top of that, I was often left in awe of the people and ideas we researched, stuff that I definitely should have known about earlier and that I can only hope we can help bring more attention to.

These are gifts I will treasure, gifts that continue to make me think, to make me question, to make me believe we can do better, for all of us. It's also been incredibly rewarding to work with a team of women, to bounce ideas off each other, to bring ideas to life via illustration, to make this whole thing happen. Last, it is an honor to have the space to share intimate pieces of ourselves with you, our readers.

SAMANTHA: Yeah, I hope you guys might be able to see the excitement we felt over the course of putting this book together, the heartbreaks we have felt— and continue to feel—given some of the setbacks that have happened recently. Overall, we want you to sense the love we have for the things we talked about in these pages, these ideas and accomplishments and goals that we are so passionate about.

And even with all the stress of writing this book, trying to figure out what to cover and how to get it all as right as we could, I can't help but feel good about our efforts. I'd like to believe we are doing something that will honor the folks who have fought so hard to bring equality to all.

I'm not gonna lie, the professionals who have helped us in the process have been amazingly supportive. Having people like you, Anney, the overachiever, always pushing me and challenging me, you gave me hope that we could actually finish this thing. Working with our brilliant illustrator, Helen Choi, has been one of the best experiences. Watching her bring our ideas to beautiful life for the graphic novel portions of this book was one of the most exciting parts of this project.

* * * * *

SAMANTHA: You know, Anney, as we've said, we've talked a lot about what it was that we were trying to do with this book, and what we hoped our readers would take away from it. And honestly, there are so many things that we had to sift through in order to figure out how to end up with a somewhat cohesive book! So many things have happened in our history, a path to progress that has been paved by such remarkable and strong women and nonbinary folks—it was such a difficult process, narrowing it all down to fit in these pages. One of the bigger struggles for me was that I kept wanting to add more people to celebrate and tell their story. But we did it, finally. Right?

ANNEY: I think we did! Yeah, one of the main takeaways for me in writing this book was this idea of inevitability. I just can't shake the idea that people who are marginalized are going to keep fighting and pushing. There are setbacks and failures, and those have impacts, both positive and negative in terms of inspiring others. But the fight is necessary—and it'll never stop. Because we don't really have the luxury to rest.

So much of this process felt like a dialogue, one that is very much still in motion, forever evolving and adapting. So much of it is asking the question: How much progress has been made? Oftentimes the answer to that question is a double-edged sword, equal parts frightening and hopeful.

A great deal of the progress we've discussed in this book is in flux as we write. The rights we've struggled to win are in danger, even after all the years and all the incredible people that fought for them. I do see a lot of growth. But I also see a lot of unknowns.

Writing this book has been enlightening as well, reckoning with what I know and what I don't know. Being a feminist is to be in a constant state of questioning things, of learning and unlearning and relearning. That is daunting, but it's also exciting, just like the process of writing this book.

Our team had many conversations about how many people have been erased, about how to keep the premise of "what if this didn't happen" respectful. We had an unfortunate awareness that some of these events aren't taught in schools, so many people might not know how to distinguish the truth from the fiction.

I learned *so much*, about so many amazing women, too many to fit in the space of this work. That's inspiring, and it gives me a sense of responsibility too—they've done the work. Now I need to honor them and highlight them and build on what they've done and are continuing to do. We all do. And I hope that this ultimately is a message of hope, an affirmation that all of us can participate in this movement. We can all make changes, no matter how small. We can all come together to create something beautiful and enormous.

SAMANTHA: Absolutely! I love that so much, that we are building hope, that we can create something beautiful, as a way to honor those who came before us and to inspire those after us. I hope that throughout the book, readers are intrigued enough to go out and dig deeper into some of these ideas, then take that inspiration and become powerhouses on their own.

The point of our book, though the path has been paved with disappointment, is that we are fighters. We may hit roadblocks, we may have uphill battles, but we are fighters through and through. We have, from the beginning, learned that in order for change to happen, we are the ones who have to take a stand.

And the generations to come will learn and be inspired from the past and will stop shrinking. We will start taking up as much space as we deserve.

Anney, we made it—we wrote a book! It feels like it took forever but somehow was also completely rushed, but we made it. Now that we are at the finish line and reflecting on the process, I'm wondering, did we accomplish what we set to do, do you think?

ANNEY: In a lot of ways, yes. We got to include our graphic novel bits (so exciting!) and illustrations, and we covered many issues that are close to our hearts. Throughout the process, we got to learn a lot, and hopefully readers will too. We covered a lot of ground. With that comes the knowledge that there's *so much* left. Perhaps a sequel is in the future, or perhaps one of you reading will continue the good work.

The primary thing I wanted to accomplish was presenting these hugely important moments, whether you'd heard of them or not, in a new light, and hammering home just how huge and significant they were, how much influence they've had on young folks everywhere. And how much hard, and often thankless, work was involved, and how all the accomplishments resulting from that work need to be protected.

I wanted people to continue to question the systems we live in and wonder how we can do better. And despite the somewhat dire topics we covered, I wanted to leave people with hope, with a sense that they can make a difference, and that if they feel alone, they aren't. I hope we have succeeded.

SAMANTHA: Agreed. I'm crossing my fingers that we have been able to translate our intentions in a way that comes across for the readers. The number of things that have happened in history and the many women and folks who have had a hand in that are extensive and overwhelming. I do hope we can highlight more (hey, we have several of those wonderful folks on our podcast, so that's the good news).

But, overall, we hope that we have given you, the readers, a new perspective, and perhaps helped you learn about new people or events, so that you can go off and find out more and talk to others about the mind-boggling things these people have accomplished.

Anney, can I just say a hearty congratulations, my dear friend? We did it and if we were recording for our podcast, I think this is the part where we would say cheers, right? And you know, we always love to end with a self-care moment. Now that we have finished our very difficult book journey, what are you going to do to reward and care for yourself?

ANNEY: This will be no surprise to anyone who knows me: the answer is fan fiction. I'm going to read a lot of it, and write a lot of it, and probably cry along the way. I'm going to drink a lot of water and stretch and try to sleep regular hours, or at least, more regular hours. Go for walks. Lie in bed and listen to classical music and stare into the galaxy of my star projector. And probably play video games.

SAMANTHA: Ooh, yes, gotta do your favorite go-tos. As for me, gonna get a glass of wine, sit on the end of my couch, cuddle my dog, Peaches, while watching my favorite comfort movies and not think for a minute.

And just so you know, Anney and readers, I am so thankful to have experienced this with all of y'all. Anney, you are amazing; I admire and love you and am so honored to be doing this with you!

ANNEY: Right back at you, Samantha. What a trip this has been!

ACKNOWLEDGMENTS

IT TAKES A VILLAGE TO WRITE A BOOK, and there have been so many people every step of the way from ideation to publication we'd like to acknowledge. We can't possibly thank them all, but here are a few.

First, this book wouldn't exist without the podcast *Stuff Mom Never Told You*, and the podcast wouldn't exist without past creators and hosts Cristen Conger, Caroline Ervin, Bridget Todd, Emilie Aries, and Molly Edmonds. These women fundamentally shaped and inspired us to continue evolving, to find our voice and our feminism. We'd also like to thank our producers and editors, Dylan Fagan, Andrew Howard, Christina Loranger, Yves Jeffcoat, Maya Howard, Joey Patt, Holly Frey, Christopher Hassiotis, and so many others who have provided encouragement and support.

Special shoutout to artist and designer Pam Peacock. Not only did she design our logo, but she also put us in touch with Helen Choi, who took our garbled words and ideas and turned them into beautiful and moving illustrations. This book would be so much lesser without her work.

To the numerous guests who have appeared on our show, know that you were instrumental in so much of what we put in this book, and we are in awe of your work. One in particular we'd like to mention is researcher Renee Shelby, whose work was hugely influential for the rape kits chapter.

Thanks also to Byrd Leavell and his excellent team at UTA, along with Zack Wagman and his wonderful colleagues at Flatiron Books in editorial, production, marketing, and sales. To Carrie Lieberman, for talking us through our many questions. And especially to Jane Fleming Fransson, who was kind, understanding, monumentally helpful, and kept us on a deadline even when we were completely lost about what the heck we were doing. This book would simply not exist without her.

I'd like to personally thank Roxanne Reid, Jeri Rowland, and Lauren Vogelbaum, who gave me a chance and provided advice and mentorship. My mom, for being steady and unwavering and just what I need when I'm afraid. The friends I'm unbelievably lucky to have and could not have done this without: Katie C., Katie S., Katelyn, Marissa, Whitney, and of course, the cohost of the show and coauthor of this book, Samantha (who, shockingly, remained my good friend through writing a book together on a tight schedule while also working together on a full-time podcast). It's been a pleasure working with you, and you've taught me so much. My sincerest thanks to those who create all the entertainment that got me through this, be it *Star Wars*, *The Last of Us*, or fanfiction.

And of course, thanks to all the intersectional feminists we highlighted— and those we didn't—who have been doing this work, who continue to do this work, and will do this work in the future. We would not be here without you, and we cannot thank you enough.

First, I would like to acknowledge the many amazing activists, world changers, historians, scientists, rebels, and fighters who have dedicated their lives, their time, and their hearts pushing for justice and equality for so many. And to those who have been overlooked or not credited for the years of labor you put in trying to make the world better, thank you. We hope to live up to the standards you have set.

To my friends and chosen family, thank you so much for the patience and support you have always provided. It's because of you that I am constantly challenged to do better and to seek better. Thank you especially to Caroline, who paved the path for me to be a part of this industry, but more importantly helped me to be more confident with sharing my voice and realizing that my voice is of value. Thanks to Joe who has been with me every step in this process, always caring for me, whether it's keeping me fed or just being the shoulder to lean on when my anxiety made me feel like everything is impossible. Thank you to those who humored me as I went down this unknown path, and who diligently and kindly brought me back to reality when I felt overwhelmed. Thank you to Anney, my cohost and close friend who has become the perfect puzzle piece in my whole process, taking up the slack when I (too often) procrastinate, humoring my ideas (whether outlandish or not), and always willing to reassure me when I felt insecure or unsure at this process.

And most importantly, our SMNTY fam, y'all have been one of the most accepting and supportive groups ever. I have felt so honored to be able to do a job that I never even dreamed of—being able to share our stories and the many stories and concepts that have shaped and continue to shape feminism. Thank you so much for sticking with us through all the changes and thank you for accepting me into the family!

SELECTED BIBLIOGRAPHY

BATTLE OF THE SEXES

"Impact of Title IX on Women's Sports." Billie Jean King Enterprises. Accessed March 6, 2023. https://www.billiejeanking.com/equality/title-ix/.

Blickenstaff, Brian. "Throwback Thursday: How a French Feminist Staged Her Own Games and Forced the Olympics to Include Women." *Vice*. August 11, 2016. Accessed March 6, 2023. https://sports.vice.com/en_us/article/xybw9k/throwback-thursday-how-a-french-feminist-staged-her-own-games-and-forced-the-olympics-to-include-women.

"Getting into the Games: Olympic Women." National Women's History Museum. August 8, 2016. Accessed March 6, 2023. https://www.womenshistory.org/articles/getting-games-olympic-women.

Wei, Maya, and Jackie Mansky. "The Rise of the Modern Sportswoman | Science." *Smithsonian Magazine*. August 18, 2016. Accessed March 6, 2023. https://www.smithsonianmag.com/science-nature/rise-modern-sportswoman-180960174/.

THE CIVIL RIGHTS MOVEMENT

Adler, Margot. "Before Rosa Parks, There Was Claudette Colvin." NPR. March 15, 2009. https://www.npr.org/2009/03/15/101719889/before-rosa-parks-there-was-claudette-colvin.

Biography Editors. "Septima Poinsette Clark." *Biography*. Updated September 1, 2020. Accessed March 6, 2023. https://www.biography.com/activist/septima-poinsette-clark.

Fields, Liz. "The story behind Nina Simone's protest song, 'Mississippi Goddam.'" *American Masters*. January 14, 2021. https://www.pbs.org/wnet/americanmasters/the-story-behind-nina-simones-protest-song-mississippi-goddam/16651/#.

"Gloria Richardson, An Influential Yet Largely Unsung Civil Rights Pioneer, Has Died." NPR. July 19, 2021. https://www.npr.org/2021/07/19/1017820962/gloria-richardson-civil-rights-pioneer-dies.

Godoy, Maria. "Meet The Fearless Cook Who Secretly Fed—And Funded—The Civil Rights Movement." NPR. January 15, 2018. https://www.npr.org/sections/thesalt/2018/01/15/577675950/meet-the-fearless-cook-who-secretly-fed-and-funded-the-civil-rights-movement.

"Greensboro Sit-In." History. Updated January 25, 2022. https://www.history.com/topics/black-history/the-greensboro-sit-in.

Mack, Dwayne. "Jo Ann Robinson (1912-1992)." BlackPast. May 30, 2009. https://www.blackpast.org/african-american-history/robinson-jo-ann-1912-1992/.

Magill, Joanna. "Black and Blue: How Nina Simone transformed the Civil Rights movement into music." *The Edge*. November 12, 2017. https://www.theedgesusu.co.uk/features/2017/11/12/black-and-blue-how-nina-simone-transformed-the-civil-rights-movement-into-music/.

Miller, Klancy. 2019. "Overlooked No More: Georgia Gilmore, Who Fed and Funded the Montgomery Bus Boycott." *New York Times*. July 31, 2019. https://www.nytimes.com/2019/07/31/obituaries/georgia-gilmore-overlooked.html.

Mohdin, Aamna. "Kimberlé Crenshaw: the woman who revolutionised feminism—and landed at the heart of the culture wars." *Guardian*. 12 November 2020. https://www.theguardian.com/society/2020/nov/12/kimberle-crenshaw-the-woman-who-revolutionised-feminism-and-landed-at-the-heart-of-the-culture-wars.

"Montgomery Bus Boycott." Stanford University Martin Luther King, Jr., Research and Education Institute. Accessed March 6, 2023. https://kinginstitute.stanford.edu/encyclopedia/montgomery-bus-boycott.

Murray, Rolland. "Moya Bailey, 'Misogynoir Transformed: Black Women's Digital Resistance.'" Brown University Center for the Study of Race and Ethnicity in America. May 18, 2021. https://www.brown.edu/academics/race-ethnicity/events/moya-bailey-%E2%80%9Cmisogynoir-transformed-black-women%E2%80%99s-digital-resistance%E2%80%9D.

Norwood, Arlisha. "Dorothy Height (1912–2010)." National Women's History Museum. 2017. Accessed March 6, 2023. https://www.womenshistory.org/education-resources/biographies/dorothy-height.

Reese, Linda W. "Clara Luper (1923–2011)." BlackPast.org. January 17, 2007. https://www.blackpast.org/african-american-history/luper-clara-1923/.

"Who Is Pauli Murray?" Pauli Murray Center. Accessed March 6, 2023. https://www.paulimurraycenter.com/who-is-pauli.

"Women's Political Council (WPC) of Montgomery." Stanford University Martin Luther King, Jr. Research and Education Institute. Accessed March 6, 2023. https://kinginstitute.stanford.edu/encyclopedia/womens-political-council-wpc-montgomery.

Worthen, Meredith. "Diane Nash." *Biography*. Updated November 16, 2021. https://www.biography.com/activist/diane-nash.

THE PANTSUIT REVOLUTION

Ross, Nancy L. "Update: First woman to wear pants on House floor, Rep. Charlotte Reid." *Washington Post*. December 24, 1969. Updated December 21, 2011. https://www.washingtonpost.com/blogs/reliable-source/post/update-first-woman-to-wear-pants-on-house-floor-rep-charlotte-reid/2011/12/21/gIQAVLD99O_blog.html.

Sears, Jocelyn. "Why Women Couldn't Wear Pants on the Senate Floor Until 1993." *Mental Floss*. March 22, 2017. https://www.mentalfloss.com/article/93384/why-women-couldnt-wear-pants-senate-floor-until-1993.

LGBTQ+ Rights and the Fight for Same-Sex Marriage

Prager, Sarah. "Where are the first lesbian couples in the world to legally marry now?" *The Lily*. March 27, 2021. Accessed March 6, 2023. https://www.thelily.com/20-years-ago-these-brides-made-lgbtq-history-where-are-they-now/.

Singh, Sejal, and Durso, Laura E. "Widespread Discrimination Continues to Shape LGBT People's Lives in Both Subtle and Significant Ways." *Center for American Progress*. May 2, 2017. Accessed March 6, 2023. https://www.americanprogress.org/article/widespread-discrimination-continues-shape-lgbt-peoples-lives-subtle-significant-ways/.

"The secret history of same-sex marriage." *Guardian*. 23 January 2015. Accessed March 6, 2023. https://www.theguardian.com/books/2015/jan/23/-sp-secret-history-same-sex-marriage.

THE HISTORY OF REPRODUCTIVE RIGHTS

Bingham, Clara. 2019. "Code Names and Secret Lives: How a Radical Underground Network Helped Women Get Abortions Before They Were Legal." *Vanity Fair*. April 17, 2019. https://www.vanityfair.com/style/2019/04/jane-network-abortion-feature.

Gaddy, Brittany N., and Kelly Livingston. Capital News Service. October 28, 2021. "Abortion bans disproportionately impact marginalized communities, activists say." https://cnsmaryland.org/2021/10/28/abortion-bans-disproportionately-impact-marginalized-communities-activists-say/.

North, Anna. "This is what it was like to perform abortions before Roe." *Vox*. May 24, 2019. https://www.vox.com/2019/5/24/18630825/abortion-roe-v-wade-vs-jane-collective.

Disability Rights: Making the Table Accessible

Carmel, Julia. "Before the A.D.A., There Was Section 504." *New York Times*. July 22, 2020. Accessed March 6, 2023. https://www.nytimes.com/2020/07/22/us/504-sit-in-disability-rights.html.

Ferrante, Dana. "Diversity & Inclusion's Learn More Series Focuses on Disability and Impact of Ableism." *BU Today*. September 13, 2021. Accessed March 6, 2023. https://www.bu.edu/articles/2021/judy-heumann-disability-rights-leader-to-speak-at-learn-more-series/.

McGreevy, Nora. "The ADA Was a Monumental Achievement 30 Years Ago, but the Fight for Equal Rights Continues." *Smithsonian Magazine*. July 24, 2020. Accessed March 6, 2023. https://www.smithsonianmag.com/history/history-30-years-since-signing-americans-disabilities-act-180975409/.

Rutherford, Beckie. "Disabled women organizing: Feminism and disability rights activism." British Library. 19 October 2020. Accessed March 6, 2023. https://www.bl.uk/womens-rights/articles/feminism-and-disability-rights-activism.

Wolfe, Kathi. "Disability Rights Group: 30 Years as a Force for Change." Disability Rights Education & Defense Fund. December 19, 2012. Accessed March 6, 2023. https://dredf.org/disability-rights-group-30-years-as-a-force-for-change/.

"Women's Disability Activism: A Timeline." Whitney Lew James. Accessed March 6, 2023. http://whitneylewjames.com/disability-activism/.

WHEN WOMEN RISE

Bailey, Megan. "Between Two Worlds: Black Women and the Fight for Voting Rights." National Park Service. Updated September 13, 2022. https://www.nps.gov/articles/black-women-and-the-fight-for-voting-rights.htm.

Biography Editors. "Amelia Boynton." *Biography*. Updated August 7, 2020. Accessed March 6, 2023. https://www.biography.com/activist/amelia-boynton.

Brammer, John Paul. "Why thousands of indigenous women have gone missing in Canada." *Vox*. July 15, 2016. https://www.vox.com/2016/7/5/12096898/missing-indigenous-women-canada.

Encyclopaedia Britannica Editors. "Eliza Wood Burhans Farnham: American reformer and writer." *Encyclopedia Britannica*. Updated December 11, 2022. Accessed March 6, 2023. https://www.britannica.com/biography/Eliza-Wood-Burhans-Farnham.

Encyclopaedia Britannica Editors. "National Organization for Women: American Organization." *Encyclopaedia Britannica*. Updated August 21, 2019. Accessed March 6, 2023. https://www.britannica.com/topic/National-Organization-for-Women.

Guerrero, Diane. "Mónica Ramírez." *Time*. February 17, 2021. Accessed March 6, 2023. https://time.com/collection/time100-next-2021/5937628/monica-ramirez.

"History of Western Civilization II. The March on Versailles." Lumen Learning. Accessed March 6, 2023. https://courses.lumenlearning.com/suny-hccc-worldhistory2/chapter/the-march-on-versailles/.

Hopkins, Ruth. "Activists Marched for Missing and Murdered Indigenous Women." *Teen Vogue*. February 15, 2018. https://www.teenvogue.com/story/activists-marched-for-missing-and-murdered-indigenous-women.

"Josephine St. Pierre Ruffin." History of American Women. Accessed March 6, 2023. https://www.womenhistoryblog.com/2015/06/josephine-st-pierre-ruffin.html.

Li, Sara. "Who Was Grace Lee Boggs, the Asian American Labor Organizer and Writer?" *Teen Vogue*. May 27, 2020. https://www.teenvogue.com/story/grace-lee-boggs-asian-american-labor-organizer-writer-og-history.

"Missing and Murdered Indigenous Women (MMIW)." Native Hope. Accessed March 6, 2023. https://www.nativehope.org/en-us/understanding-the-issue-of-missing-and-murdered-indigenous-women.

Norwood, Arlisha R. "Ida B. Wells-Barnett (1862–1931)." National Women's History Museum. 2017. Accessed March 6, 2023. https://www.womenshistory.org/education-resources/biographies/ida-b-wells-barnett.

Schudel, Matt. "Amelia Boynton Robinson, activist beaten on Selma bridge, dies at 104." *Washington Post*. August 6, 2015. https://www.washingtonpost.com/national/amelia-boynton-robinson-activist-beaten-on-selma-bridge-dies-at-104/2015/08/26/9478d25e-4c11-11e5-bfb9-9736d04fc8e4_story.html

Stull, Carolyn. "Luisa Moreno: Guatemalan-born labour organizer and civil rights activist." October 30, 2022. *Encyclopedia Britannica*. https://www.britannica.com/biography/Luisa-Moreno.

The National American Woman Suffrage Association. Library of Congress. Accessed March 6, 2023. https://www.loc.gov/collections/national-american-woman-suffrage-association/articles-and-essays/the-national-american-woman-suffrage-association/.

Wada, Kayomi. "National Association of Colored Women's Clubs, NACW (1896–)." BlackPast.org. December 29, 2008. https://www.blackpast.org/african-american-history/national-association-colored-women-s-clubs-inc-1896/.

"What is the MMIW Movement?" We R Native. Accessed March 6, 2023. https://www.wernative.org/articles/what-is-the-mmiw-movement.

"Women of All Red Nations." Women & the American Story. Accessed March 6, 2023. https://wams.nyhistory.org/growth-and-turmoil/feminism-and-the-backlash/women-of-all-red-nations/.

THE INVENTION OF RAPE KITS

Alptraum, Lux. "Opening a Pandora's box of truths about rape kits." *Vox*. Updated February 19, 2020. Accessed March 6, 2023. https://www.vox.com/the-highlight/2020/2/12/21121379/rape-kits-aliza-shvarts-safe-kits-anthem-exhibit.

Laux, Katie. "Testing of backlogged rape kits yields new insights into rapists and major implications for how sexual assaults should be investigated." *The Daily*. June 13, 2016. Accessed March 6, 2023. https://thedaily.case.edu/testing-of-backlogged-rape-kits-yields-new-insights-into-rapists-and-major-implications-for-how-sexual-assaults-should-be-investigated/.

McVey, Samantha, and Anney Reese. "Bonus Episode: Rape Kits." Produced by iHeartRadio. *Stuff Mom Never Told You*. April 16, 2019. Accessed March 6, 2023. https://omny.fm/shows/stuff-mom-never-told-you/bonus-episode-rape-kits

"National Best Practices for Sexual Assault Kits: A Multidisciplinary Approach." Office of Justice Programs. August 7, 2017. Accessed March 6, 2023. https://nij.ojp.gov/topics/articles/national-best-practices-sexual-assault-kits-multidisciplinary-approach.

Strawser, Will. "A Wrenching Dilemma." *Washington Post*. February 20, 2018. Accessed March 6, 2023. https://www.washingtonpost.com/news/style/wp/2018/02/20/feature/decades-worth-of-rape-kits-are-finally-being-tested-no-one-can-agree-on-what-to-do-next/.

About iHeartMedia

iHeartMedia is the number one audio company in the United States, reaching nine out of ten Americans every month—and with a quarter of a billion monthly listeners, it has a greater reach than any other media company in the United States. The company's leading position in audio extends across multiple platforms, including more than 850 live broadcast stations in over 160 markets nationwide; its iHeartRadio digital service available across more than 250 platforms and 2,000 devices; its influencers; social media; branded iconic live music events; other digital products and newsletters; and podcasts as the number one commercial podcast publisher. iHeartMedia also leads the audio industry in analytics, targeting, and attribution for its marketing partners with its SmartAudio product, using data from its massive consumer base. Visit iHeartMedia.com for more company information.

About the Authors

Anney Reese is a podcaster, writer, and actor. In 2014, she began hosting and producing the podcast *FoodStuff* (later rebranded as *Savor*), and in 2017, she took over as one of the hosts of the popular feminist podcast *Stuff Mom Never Told You*. Through the process of podcasting and writing, she has produced, written, and hosted over 1,000 scripts and pieces for both fiction and nonfiction, and has spoken at several podcasting conferences. She is also a huge nerd and loves writing, reading, video games, and cosplay.

Samantha McVey has always had a passion for social justice, which led her to both an education and career in social work, where she dedicated her focus to advocating for women and children in her community. In early 2019, she translated her experience and passion for social justice and women into a collaboration with the feminist podcast *Stuff Mom Never Told You* for a mini-series on trauma and the #MeToo era. Her stint was so successful, she came onto the show full time, where she provided a much-needed perspective on a whole range of issues impacting the most marginalized of people. Samantha has guested on several different podcasts and spoken at podcasting conferences around the country. She lives in Atlanta, GA with her adorable mutt, Peaches.